SCHLESWIG-HOLSTEIN

SCHLESWIG-HOLSTEIN

DEUTSCH - ENGLISCH

TEXTE / TEXTS

BRIGITTE SCHUBERT-RIESE

FOTOS / PHOTOGRAPHS

PETER SCHUSTER

ÜBERSETZUNG / TRANSLATION

GÜNTER SCHUBERT

Wachholtz Verlag

Impressum

Alle Rechte, auch die des auszugsweisen Nachdrucks,
insbesondere für Vervielfältigungen, die Einspeicherung
und Verarbeitung in elektronischen Systemen sowie
der fotomechanischen Wiedergabe und Übersetzung
vorbehalten.

ISBN 3–529–05333–3

Wachholtz Verlag 2006

Fotonachweis

Fotos, die nicht vom Bildautor stammen:
Seite 24 (THW Kiel): www.living-sports.de
Seite 74 (Damp 2000): Damp Touristik GmbH
Seite 26 (Team Pohl/Rau): Nivea (c)
Seite 95 (Kalkberg-Arena): www.nordlicht-online.de
Seite 95 (Rathaus): Uwe Paulsen
Seite 110 (historisches Lübeck): Uwe Paulsen

Historische Fotos (Seiten 9–11): Archiv Peter Schuster

Inhaltsverzeichnis / Table of Contents

Entstehung und Geschichte

Das Image Schleswig-Holsteins ist anhaltend von seiner Lage am Rand Mitteleuropas geprägt. Eine Region zwischen zwei Meeren, mit einer Staatsgrenze im Norden, vom Osten lange Zeit durch die deutsch-deutsche Grenze abgetrennt; weit entfernt von pulsierenden Metropolen und boomenden Wirtschaftszentren. Über diesen südlichen Teil der Landbrücke zwischen Mittel- und Nordeuropa wickelten sich Handel und Verkehr ab, wurden geistige und kulturelle Einflüsse aufgenommen, aber auch politische Konflikte ausgetragen. In der Gegenwart, in der die Räume durch ein zusammenwachsendes Europa neu definiert werden, fungiert Schleswig-Holstein als Drehscheibe im Ostseeraum: nach Skandinavien und in die osteuropäischen Staaten.

Origin and History

Schleswig-Holstein's image has continuously been influenced and determined by its position at the periphery of Central Europe. It is a region between two seas, with a state-border to its north, for a long time separated from the East by the German-German border, and it is far away from vibrant metropolises and booming economic centres. It was here in the southern part of the landbridge between Central- and Northern Europe that trade and traffic were concentrated, and that intellectual and cultural influences were absorbed. Also political conflicts were argued out and settled here. Currently, when areas and regions are freshly being defined as a consequence of a merging Europe, Schleswig-Holstein functions as the Baltic transit route and traffic junction to Scandinavia and the Eastern European states.

Runenstein von Bustorf / Bustorf, Rune-stone

Nydamboot, Schloss Gottorf / Nydamboat, Castle Gottorf

Langbetten „Ruserberg" bei Hohwacht (2700 - 2500 vor Christus)
Grave site "Ruserberg" near Hohwacht (2700-2500 B.C.)

Das Land zwischen Nord- und Ostsee ist von Eismassen aus Skandinavien und dem Weichselgebiet geschaffen. Als die Gletscher abgeschmolzen waren, zeigte sich die Gliederung der Landschaft: fruchtbare Marschen entlang der Nordsee und Elbe, die karge Geest auf dem Mittelrücken und das seenreiche östliche Hügelland. Megalithgräber und Funde in den Mooren zeugen von einer frühen Besiedlung. Friesen und Dänen setzten sich im Schleswiger Raum, Slawen und Sachsen im Holsteiner Gebiet fest. Unter den Karolingern wurde die Region in das Frankenreich einbezogen und von dort missioniert: Ansgar war der Apostel des Nordens. Die Eider wurde zur Grenze zwischen dem Herzogtum Schleswig und der Grafschaft Holstein-Storman. Halb deutsches, halb dänisches Lehen, geriet Nordelbien schon früh in das Spannungsfeld der großen Politik. Gegen Expansionsversuche von beiden Seiten entwickelten die Herzogtümer den starken Willen zur Zusammengehörigkeit. Die ließen sie sich bei der Wahl des dänischen Königs zum gemeinsamen Landesherrn garantieren. „Dat se bliven ewich tosamende ungedeelt", heißt es im Ripener Freiheitsbrief von 1460.

Herrschaftsteilungen und Auseinandersetzungen zwischen den regierenden Häusern bestimmten die Folgezeit. Die Eingliederung in den dänischen Gesamtstaat, zu dem u.a. Norwegen, Island und Grönland gehörten, brachte auch für Schleswig und Holstein die „Ruhe des Nordens" mit wirtschaftlicher Prosperität und kultureller Blüte; zumal Mitglieder des deutsch-dänischen Adelskreises einflussreiche

Lütjenburg: mittelalterliche Turmhügelburg (rekonstruiert)
Lütjenburg, Replica of medieval towerhill-castle

politische Positionen besetzten. Als dieser Staat in die Krise geriet, brachen - wie in ganz Europa- die Gegensätze auf. Die deutsche Nationalbewegung wollte die Herzogtümer Schleswig, Holstein und Lauenburg als Einheit in das entstehende Deutsche Reich eingegliedert wissen, die Partei der „Eiderdänen" verlangte die enge Anbindung Schleswigs an das dänische Königreich. Die schleswig-holsteinische Erhebung in dem Drei-Jahreskrieg von 1848 bis 1851 endete mit der Niederlage in der Schlacht von Idstedt.

Bosau: von Vicelin gegründete Urkirche
Bosau, Early church founded by Vicelin

Danach wurde das dänische Staatsgebilde wiederhergestellt. Die Auseinandersetzung um die Verfassung der Herzogtümer und das Erbrecht, die bereits die europäischen Kabinette beschäftigte, blieb aber virulent. Darin sah Bismarck die Chance, die Gebiete für Preußen zu gewinnen. Nach dem Sieg der preußisch-österreichischen Truppen auf den Düppeler Schanzen wurden die Herzogtümer von Dänemark abgetrennt: nach 400 Jahren war das dänisch-schleswig-holsteinische Zusammenleben zerstört. Am Ende des Krieges, den Bismarck gegen Österreich um die Vorherrschaft in Deutschland führte, wurden Schleswig und Holstein gegen den Willen der meisten Einwohner in Preußen einverleibt. Das Land wurde preußische Provinz und dann Teil des deutschen Reiches.

The land between the North Sea and the Baltic was brought into existence by masses of ice from Scandinavia and the area along the Weichsel. When

Grabmal Friedrich I. von Dänemark im Schleswiger Dom
Monument of Friedrich I. of Denmark in the Schleswig Cathedral

the glaciers had melted down, the geological division of the land became visible. There was fertile marshland alongside the North Sea and the Elbe, barren 'Geest' along the central ridge, and hilly country with an abundance of lakes to the east. Megalithic graves and archaeological finds in the moorland tell of early settlement. Frisians and Danes made their homes in the region around Schleswig, Slavs and Saxons settled in Holstein. Under the rule of the Carolingians the region was incorporated in the Franconian Empire and was converted from there. Ansgar was the Apostle of the North. The Eider became the borderline between the Duchy of Schleswig and the County of Holstein-Stormarn. Due to its being half German and half Danish, Nordelbien very quickly got involved with political conflicts. Against the attempts at expansion from both sides, the duchies developed a feeling of solidarity. This they found guaranteed by electing the Danish King their mutual sovereign. In the 'Ripen Freiheitsbrief' of 1460 it says: 'Dat se bliven ewich tosamede ungedelt'.

The following period was characterized by land partitions and confrontations between the governing Houses. The incorporation into the Danish 'Gesamtstaat', that – among others - also included Norway, Iceland, and Greenland, meant 'peace and quiet of the North' also to Schleswig-Holstein with economic prosperity and flourishing cultural life; the more so since members of the German-Danish nobility occupied influential positions. When this state met with a crisis, differences of opinion occurred like everywhere else in Europe. The German Nationalistic Movement wanted to see Schleswig, Holstein, and Lauenburg integrated as a unit in the developing German Reich, the Party of the 'Eiderdänen' insisted on the close linking up of Schleswig with the Danish kingdom. The Schleswig-Holstein uprising in the Three-Years-War of 1848 to 1851 ended with the defeat in the Battle of Idstedt.

Subsequently the Danish State was restored. However, the conflict about the constitution of the counties and the law of succession that already engrossed the European cabinets prevailed. Here Bismarck saw the chance of winning the regions for Prussia. As a consequence of the victory of the Prussian-Austrian troops on the 'Düppelner Schanzen', the dukedoms were partitioned off from Denmark. After 400 years the Danish-Schleswig-Holstein coexistence had come to an end. At the end of the war which Bismarck waged against Austria about the predominance in Germany, Schleswig and Holstein were annexed to Prussia against the will of most of the population. The land became a Prussian province and subsequently part of the German Reich.

Deutsche Flottenbegeisterung: Postkarte um 1905
German enthusiasm for the fleet, postcard about 1905

Revolutionsdenkmal von H.-J. Breuste in Kiel
Kiel, Monument to the Revolution by H.-J. Breuste

Als Deutschland im 1. Weltkrieg unausweichlich vor der militärischen Niederlage stand, setzte der Kieler Matrosenaufstand ein Signal. Der Weg führte über die Revolution und das Ende des Kaiserreichs zur Weimarer Republik. Entsprechend den Versailler Vertragsbestimmungen wurde in zwei Volksabstimmungen die Grenze zwischen Deutschland und Dänemark so festgelegt, wie sie heute verläuft. Über sie schickte der NS-Staat – dessen Entstehung die Schleswig-Holsteiner in den Wahlen zum Reichstag nachdrücklich befördert hatten – für vier Jahre Besatzungstruppen nach Kopenhagen.

Die Folgen des von Deutschland entfesselten Krieges trafen auch den Norden. Besonders Kiel und Lübeck mit ihren Rüstungsbetrieben waren Ziel der Luftangriffe. Am Ende des Krieges waren über 70 Prozent der Kieler Wohngebäude zerstört oder schwer beschädigt. Der Bombenangriff auf Lübeck in der Nacht zum Palmsonntag 1942 setzte ein Fünftel der Altstadt in Flammen. Als die letzte Reichsregierung unter Großadmiral Dönitz die Kapitulation der Wehrmacht von Mürwik aus bekannt gab, war Schleswig-Holstein bereits Zufluchtsland für die Flüchtlinge und Vertriebenen. Sie hatten sich in den letzten Kriegsmonaten vom Osten auf Schiffen und mit Trecks hierher gerettet. 1946 hatte sich die Bevölkerungszahl von 1,6 Millionen Einwohnern um eine Million Hinzugezogene erhöht.

Der Kampf gegen die Not und die Eingliederung der Flüchtlinge waren die wichtigsten Aufgaben, die sich der ersten Landesregierung des 1947 gegründeten Bundeslandes Schleswig-Holstein stellten. Der demokratische Neubeginn und der Wiederaufbau be-

stimmten die Zielrichtung. Unter dieser Vorgabe konnten nach und nach wieder Verbindungen zu anderen Ländern aufgenommen und das angespannte Verhältnis zwischen den nationalen Minderheiten diesseits und jenseits der Grenze entschärft werden. Die Bonn-Kopenhagener Erklärungen von 1955 haben ein Gleichgewicht geschaffen, das die dänische Volksgruppe in Südschleswig und die deutsche Volksgruppe in Nordschleswig in ihrer kulturellen Autonomie schützt. Die politische Vertretung der dänischen Minderheit, der SSW, ist von der 5-Prozent-Klausel im Landtagswahlrecht befreit. Diese Form des friedlichen Zusammenlebens hat für das heutige Europa Modellcharakter.

Stunde Null nach dem Krieg / Devastation after the war

Die Politik der Nachkriegszeit hatte in einem umfangreichen Modernisierungsprozess die Strukturprobleme des Flächenlandes an der Peripherie zu lösen und den Wandel von der Agrargesellschaft zur Industrie- und Dienstleistungsgesellschaft einzuleiten. In der Gegenwart geht es darum, Schleswig-Holsteins Chancen als Drehscheibe im Ostseeraum zu nutzen.

When in World War I the Reich inevitably moved towards its military defeat, the sailors' revolt ('Matrosenaufstand') in Kiel opened the way for the Revolution, for the end of the monarchy and for the Weimar Republic. In correspondence with the regulations set down in the Treaty of Versailles two referendums fixed the borderline between Germany and Denmark to where it is today. For four years the Nazi

Nissenhütten: Wohnraum für Flüchtlinge und Vertriebene
Nissenhuts, living-room for the refugees, and displaced persons

regime which had explicitly been supported by the Schleswig-Holstein population in the election for the Reichstag, sent occupying forces to Copenhagen. The horrors of the war, triggered by Germany, also hit the North. In particular Kiel and Lübeck with their armament industries were severely hit in the air-raids. At the end of the war more than 70% of the residential buildings lay in ashes or were seriously damaged. After the bomb-attack on Lübeck in the night preceding Palm Sunday in 1942, one fifth of the old part of the town was up in flames. When the last Government of the Reich under Admiral of the Fleet Dönitz from Mürwik made public the surrender of the 'Wehrmacht', Schleswig-Holstein had already become a resort for refugees and displaced persons. In the last months of the war they had escaped from the East in boats or on foot. By 1946 the total population number of 1.6 million had increased by another million.

The struggle against economic plight and the integration of the refugees were the most important tasks that in 1947 confronted the first government of the Federal State Schleswig-Holstein. The democratic fresh start and reconstruction determined the governmental targets. Under such guidelines contacts with other countries could eventually be established, and the tense relation between the national minorities on both sides of the border could be defused. The Bonn-Copenhagen-Declarations of 1955 created a balance that protects the Danish ethnic group in Southern Schleswig as well as the German population in Northern Schleswig in their respective cultural autonomy. In governmental elections the diplomatic mission of the Danish minority, the SSW, is exempt from the duty to reach 5% of the electoral votes. This form of peaceful coexistence serves as a model for today's Europe.

Political responsibility in the aftermath of the war meant solving the structural crisis of a rural area situated at the periphery by means of an extensive process of modernization, and initiating the change from an agrarian- into an industrial- and service-oriented society. Today the issue is to utilize Schleswig-Holstein's potential as a nerve-centre on the Baltic.

Schleusen Kiel-Holtenau / Kiel-Holtenau, Locks

Wirtschaft und Forschung

Leuchtende Rapsflächen, satte Weiden mit Schwarz-bunten, wogende Kornfelder zwischen dichten Knicks weisen Schleswig-Holstein als Agrarland aus, idyllische Fischerhäfen gehören in das Bild des Küstenlandes. In den traditionellen Bereichen Landwirtschaft, Fischerei und Schifffahrt, die die Wirtschaftsgeschichte der Herzogtümer geprägt haben, haben sich Strukturen gewandelt und Schwerpunkte verändert. Die Landwirte liefern nicht mehr nur qualitativ hochwertige Produkte für den Markt und die Ernährungs-industrie, sie sind mit Biogas und Rapsdiesel auch Produzenten neuer Energien und verantwortlich für den Erhalt der Kulturlandschaft und die Pflege der Umwelt. Die Flotte der Seefischerei ist geschrumpft. Fanggründe sind weggefallen, Fangquoten und – verbote wurden erlassen. Die Küstenfischerei an der Nordsee lebt von Krabbenfang und Muschelfischerei. Auf dem Vormarsch sind Aquakulturanlagen, die gezielte Fischzucht an Land ermöglichen.

Lindenau Werft: Stapellauf Doppelhüllentanker / Lindenau shipyard, Launching a double-hull-tanker

U-Boot von HDW / Submarine built by HDW

Strukturwandel ist auch das Stichwort für den Schiffbau im Lande. Die Werften haben sich auf den Bau von Container-, Spezialschiffen und U-Booten konzentriert und die Position auf dem Weltmarkt durch Innovationen gesichert: die Entwicklung des Doppelhüllentankers bei Lindenau oder der Bau des ersten U-Boots mit Brennstoffzellen-Antrieb bei den Howaldtswerken sind Beispiele. MaK-Schiffsmotoren treiben Schiffe auf allen Meeren an. Die Dieselloks laufen über die europäischen Schienennetze.

Eine Pole-Position hat das Land Schleswig-Holstein in der Meeresforschung und Meerestechnik. Das Leibniz-Institut für Meereswissenschaften IFM GEOMAR in Kiel ist ein Zentrum von Weltrang. In internationalen Projekten werden alle Bereiche der modernen Meeresforschung von der Geologie des Meeresbodens bis zur maritimen Meteorologie bearbeitet. Von der Grundlagenforschung profitieren die Anwendungsbereiche von der Medizin bis zur Offshore-Windanlage.

Betriebe aus den Sparten Umwelt-, Medizin- und Energietechnik, der Biotechnologie, aber auch der Informations- und Kommunikationstechnik produ-

zieren in Schleswig-Holstein und geben dem früheren Agrarland ein neues Wirtschaftsprofil. Das Lübecker Traditionsunternehmen Dräger gehört zu den Weltmarktführern auf dem Gebiet der Medizin- und Sicherheitstechnik. Itzehoe bietet mit dem Innovationszentrum (IZET) ein Netzwerk für Mikrotechnologien. Flaggschiff ist hier das Fraunhofer Institut für Siliziumtechnologie (ISIT) mit der Entwicklung des elektrischen Biochips. Grundlage ist jeweils der enge Austausch zwischen Wissenschaft und Wirtschaft.

Der ist in Schleswig-Holstein mit einer gut gegliederten Hochschullandschaft (neun staatliche und drei private Einrichtungen) gegeben. Forschung und Lehre an der 1665 gegründeten Christian-Albrechts-Universität in Kiel, der Medizinischen Universität Lübeck und der Universität Flensburg als bildungswissenschaftlicher Hochschule werden ergänzt durch die unterschiedlichen Kompetenzbereiche der Fachhochschulen in Kiel, Lübeck, Flensburg und Heide: Das Spektrum reicht von Technik bis Tourismus. Die Musikhochschule in Lübeck und die Mutesius Kunsthochschule in Kiel sind angesehene Adressen in der Kulturszene. Private Gründungen stärken den Wissenschaftsstandort Schleswig-Holstein.

Leibniz-Institut IFM-Geomar

Auf dem Gebiet der Wirtschaftswissenschaft und – politik hat das Institut für Weltwirtschaft mit höchstem internationalen Renommee das Profil des Landes bestimmt. Es gehört zu den sechs bedeutenden Wirtschaftsforschungsinstituten in Deutschland und hat mit seiner Bibliothek die weltweit größte Fachbibliothek für volkswirtschaftliche Literatur.

Für das Land zwischen den Meeren mit einer Küstenlänge von etwa 1.200 km ist der Küstenschutz eine elementare Aufgabe. Fast ein Viertel der Landesfläche gehört zu den Gebieten, die durch Überflutung gefährdet sind. Wesentliche Funktionen im Risikomanagement haben das GKSS-Institut für Küstenforschung (IfK) in Brunsbüttel mit dem Forschungsschwerpunkt „Lebensraum Küste" und das Forschungs- und Technologiezentrum Westküste (FTZ) in Büsum.

Economy and Scientific Research

Flowering rape fields, rich meadows with grazing Frisian cows, and swaying cornfields between dense 'Knicks' (earthwork surmounted by hedges) characterize Schleswig-Holstein as an agrarian region, and idyllic fishing-ports support the image of a coastal area. In the traditional fields like agriculture, fishing- and shipbuilding industry which together determined the economic history of the dukedoms, structures and prior-

ities have changed. No longer do farmers solely provide high-quality products for the market and food industry. With biogas and rape-diesel fuel they today also produce new energies and are responsible for the preservation of the landscape and the protection of the environment. The fishing-fleet has shrunk due to the loss of fishing grounds, the setting of fishing quotas and prohibitions. Inshore fishing on the North Sea lives off crabbing and mussel fishing. Gaining ground are aquaculture-plants that allow planned fish farming on land.

Structural change is also the catchword within the region's shipbuilding industry. Shipyards have concentrated on the construction of container- and special

Kiel: Industrie- und Handelskammer
Kiel, Chamber of Industry and Commerce

Institut für Weltwirtschaft Kiel
Kiel, Institute for the World Economy

purpose-ships and also on submarines. Their position on the international market has been secured by innovations such as the development of the double-hull-tanker at the Lindenau Yard or the construction of the first submarine with fuel-cell propulsion at HDW. MaK-motors are powering ships on all the seas, its Diesel-locomotives are running on all European railway networks.

Itzehoe: Fraunhofer-Institut ISIT

When it comes to marine research and maritime technology, Schleswig-Holstein is holding pole-position. The Leibniz-Institute for Marine Research (IFM GEO-MAR) in Kiel is a centre of high international reputation. International projects cover all aspects of modern marine research from the geology of the bottom of the sea to maritime meteorology. Fields of application such as medicine and offshore wind-farms are profiting from this fundamental research.

Firms involved with such branches as environmental-, medical-, and energy-technology, in bio-technology and also in information- and communication-technol-

ogy are producing in Schleswig-Holstein and have given the former agrarian region a new economic profile. The traditional firm Dräger in Lübeck ranks worldwide among the market leaders in medical- and security-technology. Itzehoe with its innovation centre (IZET) offers a network of micro-technologies. Flagship here is the Fraunhofer Institute for Silicon Technology (ISIT) with the development of the electric biochip. Basic component throughout is the close contact between science and economy.

This contact is guaranteed in Schleswig-Holstein by its well-structured higher education system, with nine state- and three private institutions. Research and teaching at the Christian-Albrechts-University (1665), the Medical University in Lübeck, and at the University of Flensburg with its emphasis on educational subjects are supplemented by the different areas of authority of the Colleges (Fachhochschulen) in Kiel, Lübeck, Flensburg, and Heide, which range from technology to tourism. The Academy of Music in Lübeck and the 'Muthesius Kunsthochschule' in Kiel are distinguished addresses within the cultural scene. Private foundations add to the quality of scientific research in Schleswig-Holstein.

In the field of economics and economic policy the Kiel Institute for the World Economy with its superb international reputation has moulded the profile of Schleswig-Holstein. It is one if the six important Institutes for Economic Research in Germany. In its library it houses the most extensive media-collection in the field of economics world-wide.

Küstenschutz: Lahnungen / Coastal protection

In the face of a coastal line of about 1200 kilometres, the protection of the coast is a fundamental task throughout the region. Almost a quarter of the countryside is in danger of being flooded. Essential functions in the risk-management lie with the GKSS-Institute for Coastal Research (IfK) in Brunsbüttel with its focus on coastal living-space and the Research and Technology Centre (FTZ) in Büsum.

Ein traditioneller Wirtschaftsfaktor an den Küsten wie im Binnenland ist der Tourismus. Standort und Klima haben Schleswig-Holstein zum beliebten Urlauberland gemacht. Die Verbindung von Erholung mit Gesundheit und Wellness, Naturerfahrung und Kulturerlebnissen lässt hohe Zuwachsraten erwarten.

Dienstleistungen, Verarbeitendes Gewerbe sowie Handel und Verkehr sind die Pfeiler in der Wirtschaft des Landes. Die Häfen und Umschlagplätze an der Ostküste haben von frühester Zeit an die Entwicklung der Region bestimmt. Die Öffnung Osteuropas und die Erweiterung der Europäischen Union hat neue Perspektiven eröffnet. Über den Nord-Ostsee-Kanal, der meistbefahrenen künstlichen Wasserstraße der Welt, ist der gesamte Ostseeraum mit den Märkten der Weltschifffahrt verbunden. Die Häfen Lübeck und Kiel sind für den Ausbau des Handels ge-

rüstet. Basis sind die Fähr-Verbindungen, die Personen und Güter z.B. nach Oslo, Göteborg, Helsinki, St. Petersburg, Tallin, Klaipeda bringen. Einen Boom löst die Flotte der Kreuzfahrer aus, mit der immer mehr Traumschiffe an den Terminals festmachen.

Das zentrale Zukunftsprojekt ist die Transitstrecke A 20, die einmal von Russland nach Frankreich führen wird. Eine durchgehende Ost-Westverbindung und eine neue Elbquerung bei Glückstadt sollen die Hamburger Metropolregion stärken und die Infrastruktur im Lande verbessern. Nach Norden ergibt sich mit der Realisierung der festen Querung des Fehmarnbelts eine direkte Anbindung an die Øresund-Region Malmø/Kopenhagen. Mit der Erweiterung der europäischen Gemeinschaft haben sich die Räume und ihre Zuordnungen verändert. Der Norden hat im künftigen Europa nur als gemeinsame Region der fünf Bundesländer Schleswig-Holstein, Mecklenburg-Vorpommern, Hamburg, Niedersachsen und Bremen Gewicht. Als Mitgift für die künftige Entwicklung kann das nördlichste Bundesland die Kompetenzen eines maritimen Zentrums, Erfahrungen in den Bereichen Windenergie und Küstenschutz, das Minderheiten-Modell der Grenzregion und die traditionellen kulturellen Kontakte in den Ostseeraum einbringen.

Internationale Schiffsverbindungen / International shipping connections

Tourism has always been a traditional economic factor along the coast as well as inland. Its location and climate have made Schleswig-Holstein a favourite resort for vacationists. The combination of recreation, health and wellness, unspoilt nature and cultural events suggests good growth rates in the future.

Service industries, manufacturing companies, as well as trade and traffic are the pillars of the region's economy. Ports and trading centres along the Eastern Coast have always determined the development of the area. The opening up of Eastern Europe and the growth of the European Union have provided new perspectives. The Kiel-Canal, the busiest man-made waterway in the world links the entire Baltic region with worldwide shipping markets. The ports of Lübeck and Kiel are prepared for the further expansion of trade.
Of fundamental importance are the ferry connections that, for instance, carry people and goods to Oslo, Gothenburg, Helsinki, St.Petersburg, Tallin or Klaipeda. A boom has been started by the fleet of cruise liners. More and more such luxury ships are mooring alongside the quays.

Focus of attention in the future will be the transit route A 20 that some day will bridge the distance from Russia to France. A straight connection from the east to the west and a new fixed link across the Elbe near Glückstadt are meant to give extra support to the Hamburg metropolitan region and to improve the area's infrastructure. To the north a direct link with the Øresund-region Malmø / Copenhagen comes as a result of the realization of the Fehmarn-Belt fixed link. The growth of the European Community has brought with it significant changes to the areas and their inter-relations.

Only as joint region of the five Federal States Schleswig-Holstein, Hamburg, Lower Saxony, Bremen, and Mecklenburg-Western Pomerania will the North be able to secure its influence and importance in the time to come. As a dowry for the future development, the northernmost Federal State can contribute its competence as a maritime centre, its experience in the fields of wind-power and coastal protection, its minority-model along the border region, and the traditional contacts with the countries situated at the Baltic Sea.

Kultur und Events

Die Lage am Rande Mitteleuropas, an dem sich die Kulturwege kreuzten, machte Schleswig-Holstein zur Stätte des Austauschs zwischen Mittel- Nord- und Osteuropa. Der früheste nordeuropäische Siedlungsplatz Haithabu ist dafür ein Beispiel; später die Hansestadt Lübeck mit ihren Kontakten weit in den Ostseeraum. Der Gottorfer Hof erreichte unter Friedrich III. internationales Ansehen. In der Ära des dänischen Gesamtstaats profitierten Künstler und Wissenschaftler in den Herzogtümern von der Metropole Kopenhagen. In der Region bildeten sich eigene Zentren: die Eutiner Residenz wurde zum Weimar des Nordens, der Emkendorfer Adelssitz war ein Musenhof und die Kieler Universität politischer und geistiger Mittelpunkt des Landes. Mit dem Aufkommen nationalstaatlicher Ideen im 19. Jahrhundert wurde der Horizont enger, die Kulturlandschaft blieb auf sich selbst verwiesen und war anfällig für den Ungeist des Nationalsozialismus.

Nach dem Zusammenbruch des Dritten Reiches galt es, das Fundament für den demokratischen Neubeginn zu legen. Der geistige und kulturelle Wiederaufbau wurde gefördert durch Partnerschaften mit England, Frankreich und den nordischen Ländern. Aber auch mit den östlichen Staaten im Ostseeraum, in dem Kunst und Kultur eng verflochten sind, entwickelten sich Verbindungen. Städtefreundschaften wurden begründet und Kontakte zwischen den Ländern geknüpft. So entstanden die Nordischen Filmtage in Lübeck und die „ars baltica", ein kulturelles Netzwerk der Ostsee-Anrainer, für das Schleswig-Holstein Ausgangspunkt war. Internationale Begegnungen erschließt das Schleswig-Holstein Musik Festival, das im Sommer Schlösser und Scheunen zu Konzertsälen macht. Hier sind die etablierten Stars zu Gast, in der von Leonard Bernstein begründeten Orchesterakademie auf Salzau trifft sich die jeunesse musicale aus aller Welt. Eine Attraktion für Opernfreunde sind die Festspiel-Aufführungen auf der Bühne im Eutiner Schlosspark. Als open air- Veranstaltungen haben die Karl-May-Festspiele in Bad Segeberg, Jazz-, Rock- und Popfestivals ihre Fans.

Emkendorf: Schleswig-Holstein-Musikfestival auf dem Lande
Emkendorf, Schleswig-Holstein-Music festival in the countryside

Culture and Events

Due to its position at the periphery of Central Europe where the various cultural trends used to meet, Schleswig-Holstein became the site of the interchange between Central-, Northern-, and Eastern Europe. The earliest north-European settlement, Haithabu, may serve as an example here, also the Hanseatic town of Lübeck with its far-reaching contacts into the Baltic sphere. Under Friedrich III the Gottorf Court gained international esteem. During the era of the Danish 'Gesamtstaat' artists and scientists in the dukedoms profited from the metropolis Copenhagen. Within the region a number of independent centres emerged: the Eutin Residence became the 'Weimar of the North', the seat of the aristocracy in Emkendorf was a 'Temple of the Muses', and Kiel University featured as the political and intellectual centre point of the state. The emergence of nation-state ideas in the 19th century narrowed the horizon, cultural life was thrown back on its own resources and was thus susceptible to the evil spirit of National Socialism.

After the collapse of the Third Reich it became necessary to lay anew the foundation of a democratic beginning. Intellectual and cultural reconstruction was supported not only by partnership with England, France, and the Nordic countries, but also by contacts with the eastern states along the Baltic, where art and culture are intricately related. Twin cities were established and contacts among the states were arranged. In this way the Nordic Film Days in Lübeck came into being and also the 'ars baltica', a cultural network among the neighbouring Baltic states, which started in Schleswig-Holstein. The Schleswig-Holstein Music Festival opens up opportunities for international social intercourse. Each summer it turns castles and barns into concert halls. Here the famous stars are invited. In the Orchestra Academy in Salzau, founded by Leonard Bernstein, the 'jeunesse musicale' from all over the world comes together. Attractions for lovers of the opera are the Festival productions on the stage in the castle grounds in Eutin. As open-air-events the Karl May-Festival in Bad Segeberg and the Jazz-, Rock-, and Pop-Festivals have their respective fan-communities.

Feldsteinkirche Ülsby / Ülsby, Fieldstone church

Typical features of the landscape are the churches that range from plain village churches, built of tufa or fieldstone, to the cathedrals in Schleswig, Lübeck, and Ratzeburg. It was from here that red-brick-building spread over the entire area of the Baltic. Their at times elaborate interiors and the instruments of famous organ-builders like Schnitger or Stellwagen are of special artistic value. Evidence for the agrarian background of the region can be found in windmills, farmhouses thatched with reed, and courtyards which have been preserved in many forms. Stately homes and castles document the aristocratic side of the area's culture.

Salzau: Schleswig-Holstein Musik Festival, Flaggenparade
Salzau, Schleswig-Holstein Musik Festival, Flag parade

Opernhaus Kiel / Kiel, Opera house

Theater und Orchester haben in Kiel und Lübeck feste Spielstätten: Carl Zuckmayer, Bernhard Minetti, Hans Söhnker, Wilhelm Furtwängler, Christoph von Dohnanyj und Klaus Tennstedt haben hier Spuren hinterlassen.
Das Landestheater ist in Flensburg, Schleswig und Rendsburg beheimatet und zeigt seine Produktionen an vielen Orten im Lande. Privatbühnen, Instrumental-Ensembles und Chöre ergänzen das Angebot.

An vielen Stellen lassen sich Geschichte und Vorgeschichte des Landes entdecken: am Danewerk – dem größten Bodendenkmal Nordeuropas – am Oldenburger Wall, im Archäologischen Zentrum Albersdorf, oder im Archäologischen Landesmuseum Schloss Gottorf.

In über 100 Museen und Sammlungen ist der Kanon der Kunst und Kulturgeschichte des Landes bewahrt. Orientierungspunkte sind das Landesmuseum Schloss Gottorf, das St. Annen-Museum in Lübeck, die Kunsthalle in Kiel und der Museumsberg in Flensburg, sowie das Freilichtmuseum in Molfsee. Galerien und Künstlerhäuser spiegeln die aktuellen Entwicklungen. Ausbildungsstätte für bildende Künstler ist die Muthesius Kunsthochschule in Kiel.

Berühmte Namen sind mit Schleswig-Holstein verbunden: Der erste deutsche Nobelpreisträger für Literatur, der Historiker Theodor Mommsen aus Garding, Theodor Storm (Husum), Friedrich Hebbel (Wesselburen), Klaus Groth (Heide), Heinrich und Thomas Mann, mit dem Nobelpreis ausgezeichnet wie der Wahl-Lübecker Günter Grass. Die Maler Emil Nolde, Ernst Barlach und Christian Rohlfs sind im

Land geboren, Vater und Sohn Hans Olde und der Kirchenmusiker Dietrich Buxtehude. Bedeutende Persönlichkeiten des Kultur- und Geisteslebens haben hier gewirkt. Die holsteinische Schweiz, Fehmarn, Sylt, die Ostsee zogen Maler an, in Ekensund bei Flensburg bildete sich eine Künstlerkolonie.

Wesentliche Anstöße bekommt die Kulturlandschaft aus der Tradition der Dänen und Friesen. Erforscht wird sie im Nordfriesischen Institut in Bredstedt. Die Sprache der Minderheiten ist im Norden und an der Westküste so präsent wie das Plattdeutsche im ganzen Land. Vielfalt entwickelt sich an den Treffpunkten, an denen sich Angehörige unterschiedlicher Kulturkreise, Zugewanderte und Einheimische begegnen. Dieser Austausch gehört in das Profil des Landes wie die traditionellen Feste, in denen sich regionale Eigenart spiegelt. Der Kieler Umschlag, die Lauenburger Schifferhöge, das Lübecker Altstadtfest, die Holstenköste in Neumünster, das Ringreiten auf Eiderstedt oder der Marner Karneval sind prominente Beispiele mit großer Resonanz.

Kunsthalle zu Kiel
Art Gallery Kiel

Hans Kock: 'Eine Rose für Charly Rivel'
Hans Kock, 'A rose for Charly Rivel '

Hans Kock Stiftung Gut Seekamp bei Schilksee
Gut Seekamp near Schilksee, Hans Kock Foundation

Theodor Storms Arbeitszimmer im Storm-Haus, Husum
Husum, Theodor Storm's study in the Storm-House

Theatres and orchestras have their permanent play houses in Kiel and Lübeck. Carl Zuckmayer, Bernhard Minetti, Hans Söhnker, Wilhelm Furtwängler, Klaus Tennstedt and Christoph von Dohnanyi left their traces here. The 'Landestheater' has its home in Flensburg, Schleswig and Rendsburg and performs in places across the country. Private companies, instrumental groups and choirs are supplementing the programme.

In various places traces of Schleswig-Holstein's history and pre-history can be detected, for instance at the 'Danewerk', the most extensive archaeological monument of northern Europe, at the Oldenburg Wall, in the Archaeological Centre Albersdorf, or else in the 'Archaeologisches Landesmuseum Schloss Gottorf'.

The canon of the art and cultural history of the region is being preserved in more than 100 museums and collections. Relevant landmarks are the 'Landesmuseum Schloss Gottorf', the 'St. Annen-Museum' in Lübeck, the 'Kunsthalle' in Kiel, the 'Museumsberg' in Flensburg, and the 'Freilichtmuseum' in Molfsee. Galleries and art-studios are mirroring contemporary developments. Training centre for artists is the 'Muthesius Kunsthochschule' in Kiel.
Famous names are associated with Schleswig-Holstein. There is the first German Nobel-prize winner for literature, the historian Theodor Mommsen from

Garding, there are Theodor Storm (Husum), Friedrich Hebbel (Wesselburen), Klaus Groth (Heide), Heinrich and Thomas Mann, the latter Nobel-prize winner like Günter Grass, Lübeck resident of his own free choice. The artists Emil Nolde, Ernst Barlach, and Christian Rohlfs were born here, also Hans Olde, father and son, and the composer of sacred music, Dietrich Buxtehude. Outstanding personalities of cultural and intellectual life worked here. The 'Holsteinische Schweiz', Fehmarn, Sylt, the Baltic... they all attracted artists, and in Ekensund near Flensburg an artists' colony emerged.

The tradition of the Danes and Frisians provided substantial impulse to the cultural scene. It is being studied in the 'Nordfriesisches Institut' in Bredstedt. Minority languages are kept alive in the north and along the west-coast, like , for instance, Low German (Plattdeutsch) in the entire region. Diversity emerges where members of different cultural backgrounds, newcomers and local people meet. This interchange is part of the region's profile, just like the traditional festivities that mirror peculiar characteristics of the area. The 'Kieler-Umschlag', the 'Schifferhöge' in Lauenburg, the Lübeck 'Altstadtfest', the 'Holstenköste' in Neumünster, the 'Ringreiten' on Eiderstedt, or the 'Karneval' in Marne... all these are outstanding examples that evoke considerable interest.

Epitaph Oldenswort (1591): Friesentracht
Epitaph Oldenswort, Frisian garb

Malerin / Painter

Happy Schwale Jazzband

Brassband: Jazzfestival Plön

Sport und Erholung

Dass Wassersport die Liste der Sportarten in Schleswig-Holstein anführt, ist nicht verwunderlich: das einzige Bundesland, das zwischen zwei Meeren liegt, hat eine Küstenlinie von etwa 1200 Kilometern, Flüsse, die fast so lang sind wie der halbe Erdumfang, und Hunderte von Seen. So stehen Ruderer aus dem Olympiastützpunkt in Ratzeburg, Segler und Surfer auf olympischen Siegertreppen; Beachvolleyballer spielen auf internationaler Tour, Kanuten und Schwimmer holen Meistertitel. Die Hochseesegler runden während der Nordseewoche Helgoland, Jollen und Yachten sind bei der Travemünder Woche am Start, und um Titel und Pokale kämpfen Teilnehmer aus 50 Nationen beim weltgrößten Segelfestival, der Kieler Woche. Wenn die Brandung vor Sylt steht, steigt die Surfer-Elite auf die Bretter. Aber das Wasser ist nicht nur für Profis da: Segeltörns, Surfen, Wasserski, Paddeltouren, Baden, Angeln, Schiffsausflüge und Bootsfahrten gehören in den Freizeitkatalog für Einheimische und Gäste.

Auf den Koppeln des Landes weiden vom Island-Pony bis zur Trakehner-Stute Pferde jeder Größe. Die wohl älteste deutsche Pferderasse – der Holsteiner – kommt aus den Marschgebieten der Elbe. Aus dem Arbeitspferd wurde durch systematische Zucht, die heute in Elmshorn beheimatet ist, ein vielseitiges Sportpferd. Der berühmteste Holsteiner, der Wallach Meteor, gewann unter dem Springreiter Fritz Tiedemann drei Mal Olympia- Medaillen. Ihm ist in Kiel ein Denkmal gesetzt. Elmshorn und Bad Segeberg sind Hochburgen des Pferdesports; Neumünster mit dem Internationalen Reitturnier und Kiel mit der Baltic Horse Show setzen Highlights. In den Ställen, auf Bauern- und Reiterhöfen wird aufgesattelt zu Ausritten und Wanderungen.

Schleswig-Holstein kann man auf dem Pferderücken erkunden, aber auch auf dem Fahrradsattel. Ein Stück des längsten Radfernwegs der Welt, die North Sea Cycle Route, führt von Klanxbüll bis an die Elbe. An der Ostseeküste reicht die Strecke von Flensburg bis Usedom. Ochsenweg und Alte Salzstraße sind historische Trassen, der Weg längs des Nord-Ostsee-Kanals garantiert ebenes Gelände, Touren an der Elbe, durch die Holsteinische Schweiz oder Lauenburg bieten Kultur- und Naturerlebnisse.Die abwechslungsreiche Landschaft ist ein ideales Revier für Jogger, Wanderer, Walker und Nordic Walker. Für sie sind an vielen Orten eigene Parcours eingerichtet worden, die untereinander verknüpft sind. In natürlichem Gelände ziehen auch die Golfer ihre Bags über gepflegte Fairways zu den Abschlägen. Der einst elitäre Sport ist längst populär, neue Plätze werden eröffnet.

Entspannung und Erholung sind Schlüsselbegriffe in dem großen Wellness - Angebot der Region. Für ein Wochenende, Urlaub oder Kur können Körper und Seele in modernen Einrichtungen aufgetankt werden. Abwechslung bieten Tiergärten, Freizeit- und Erlebnisparks in allen Landesteilen. Ski und Rodeln sind nicht gerade die Domäne der Nordlichter: aber bei ausreichend Schnee zieht es die Abfahrtfreaks zu dem einzigen Skilift, der auf den 168 m hohen Bungsberg führt.

Als Spitzensport hat sich im Lande der Handball etabliert. Wenn die Lokalmatadoren von der SG Flensburg-Handewitt und dem THW Kiel auflaufen, lassen die Fans die Hallen beben: nicht nur, wenn es um die deutsche Meisterschaft oder die Champions League geht.

Ostseehalle Kiel: Handballklassiker
THW gegen SG Flensburg-Handewitt / Handball-derby

Reiten an der Kieler Bucht / Horse-riding at the Kieler Bucht

Kite-Surfen St. Peter-Ording / Kite-surfing

Beach Volleyball – Team Pohl-Rau

Sport and Recreation

It is by no means surprising that in Schleswig-Holstein water-sports play a prominent role on the list of sports-events.As the only one of the 16 Federal States that is situated between two seas, it boasts a coastline of roughly 1200 kilometres, rivers almost as long as half the circumference of the earth, and hundreds of lakes. No wonder rowers from the Olympic Training Centre in Ratzeburg, yachtsmen and windsurfers can be found standing on the Olympic Winners' Rostrum. Beachvolleyballers take part in international tournaments, .canoeists and swimmers gain championship titles. During the North-Sea-Week, offshore yachtsmen sail around Helgoland, dinghies and yachts participate in the Travemünde Week, and in the biggest world-wide sailing event, Kiel Week, competitors from 50 nations compete with each other to win the titles and cups. When the surf is good on the island of Sylt, the windsurfer elite gets on their boards. But, of course, water is not just an affair for professionals: sailing cruises, windsurfing, water-skiing, canoeing, swimming, fishing, boat trips are on the recreational agenda for the local people as well as for their guests.

Horses of all sizes and breeds, from the Iceland pony to the Trakehner mare, are grazing on the region's pastureland. The presumably oldest German breed, the 'Holsteiner' originates in the marshlands of the Elbe. Systematic breeding, located today especially in Elmshorn, has turned this work-horse into a multipurpose racing-horse. The best-known 'Holsteiner' gelding, Meteor, won three Olympic show-jumping medals under his rider Fritz Tiedemann. In his honour

Kiel has put up a monument. Elmshorn and Bad Segeberg are strongholds of horse-racing, but also Neumünster with its International Horse Show, and Kiel with its Baltic Horse Show provide their own equestrian highlights.In all the stables and stud-farms horses are being saddled for riding-tours in the surrounding areas.

Schleswig-Holstein can be explored on horseback, but also by bicycle. A part of the longest long-distance cycle track, the North Sea Cycle Route, stretches from Klanxbüll to the Elbe. Along the Baltic coastline the route goes from Flensburg to Usedom. Ox-trail and Old Salt Road are historical routes. On the trip along the Kiel-Canal level roads are guaranteed. Tours along the Elbe, in the area of the 'Holsteinische Schweiz', or in Lauenburg provide plenty of cultural experiences and opportunities for nature studies. The great diversity of the landscape is an ideal area for joggers, hikers, and Nordic walkers. Special tracks that are linked with each other have been opened for them in many places. In unspoilt terrain golfers are carrying their bags across well-kept fairways towards the tees. This sport, until recently branded as elitist, has since become popular. New courses are constantly being opened.

Relaxation and recreation are key-concepts on the region's considerable wellness-programmes. For just a weekend, or else during one's vacation or in the form of a cure, body and soul can be re-charged in modern leisure facilities. Interesting entertainment is provided in animal-, amusement- and adventure-parks throughout the state.

Skiing, bobsleighing and luge-riding obviously are not the domain of the Northerners. However, in case of sufficient snow, the ski-freaks feel drawn to Schleswig-Holstein's only ski-lift that takes them up 168 metres on the Bungsberg.

Number one sport in the region, however, is handball. Whenever the two top local teams, the SG Flensburg-Handewitt and the THW Kiel, compete, their fanatical supporters' enthusiasm makes the sports-arenas shake...and this not only in those cases where the German Title or the Champions' League are at stake.

Radfahren am Deich / Cycling on the dyke

Schwentinefahrt / Trip on the Schwentine

Golfplatz Kitzeberg / Kitzeberg, Golf course

Zoobesuch / Visit at the Zoo

SCHLESWIG-HOLSTEIN

Größe / Size	16.000 km²
Einwohnerzahl	2,8 Millionen (ca)
Landeshauptstadt	Kiel

SCHLESWIG-HOLSTEIN

Size of the country	16.000 sq. kilometres
Population	2,8 million ca.
State capital	Kiel

Reise durchs Land

Vier schleswig-holsteinische Landkreise grenzen an die Metropole Hamburg und verweisen auf die engen Verflechtungen, die für die Entwicklung des gesamten Nordens hoch aktuell sind. Sie waren schon in der Geschichte bedeutsam. **Wedel** *markiert den Endpunkt des Weges, auf dem seit dem 14. Jahrhundert jährlich bis zu 50.000 Ochsen von Jütland durch Schleswig-Holstein bis an die Elbe getrieben wurden. Zu dem Ochsenmarkt kamen Aufkäufer von weit her, bis aus Westeuropa. Die Rolandsfigur auf dem Marktplatz kündete den Marktfrieden. Der bis ins 19. Jahrhundert florierende Handel war die Grundlage für das Wachstum der Stadt. Hier steht das Geburtshaus von Ernst Barlach. Es ist ein Museum, in dem an den Bildhauer, Grafiker und Dramatiker erinnert wird, der zu den herausragenden norddeutschen Künstlerpersönlichkeiten zählt.*

Fachwerkhaus / Half-timbered house

A tour of Schleswig-Holstein

Four Schleswig-Holstein rural districts border on Hamburg, the local metropolis. This in itself suggests the close interrelationship which is of vital interest to the entire north of Germany. The close involvement dates far back in history. **Wedel** marks the end of the trail along which since the 14th century annually up to 50.000 oxen were driven from Jutland across Schleswig-Holstein to the river Elbe. Buyers from as far as western Europe came to this ox-market. The Roland-statue on the market square stood for peace during the time of market.Until far into the 19th century this flourishing trade provided the basis for the growth of the town. Here Ernst Barlach's birthplace can also be visited. It is a museum reminiscent of the sculptor, graphic artist, and dramatist who belongs among the outstanding artists in the north of Germany.

Rolanddenkmal / Roland-statue

Willkomm-Höft: Ehemalige
Kapitäne geben Informationen
zu den Schiffen

Willkomm-Höft,
Former captains provide
information about the ships

Als holsteinischer Elbehafen hatte Wedel in der Vergangenheit wirtschaftliche Bedeutung. Heute lockt das Ufer als Naherholungsgebiet. Eine Attraktion für Binnenländer ist das Schulauer Fährhaus mit der Schiffsbegrüßungsanlage „Willkomm-Höft".

*Über die Pinnau mit der Elbe verbunden wuchs die Stadt **Uetersen** zum wichtigen Binnenhafen. An die Gründungszeit erinnert das Kloster, das im Laufe der Reformation - wie die Einrichtungen von Itzehoe, Preetz und Johannis vor Schleswig - in ein adliges Damenstift umgewandelt wurde. Die Kirche aus dem Spätbarock hat in dem Deckenfresco ein künstlerisches Kleinod. Im Sommer zieht ein Blütenmeer Rosenfreunde in das Rosarium.*

Weitläufige Baumschulen bestimmen das Landschaftsbild des Kreises Pinneberg. Aus dem Sortiment von 200.000 Artikeln decken Kunden von Skandinavien bis Fernost ihren Bedarf: Hobby- und Landschaftsgärtner, Obstbauern, Forstwirte oder Betreiber von Gartencentern.

As a Holstein port on the Elbe Wedel was of considerable economic significance .Today the river banks attract people as a recreation area. One attraction for inlanders is the 'Schulauer Fährhaus' with 'Willkomm-Höft', where incoming ships are given a friendly welcome.

Connected across the Pinnau with the Elbe , the town of **Uetersen** grew to be an important river port. The monastery that – like the institutions in Itzehoe, Preetz, and Johannis near Schleswig – was during the Reformation turned into an aristocratic convent reminds visitors of the foundation days. With its ceiling fresco the late-Baroque church owns an artistic gem. During the summer a sea of blossoms lures lovers of roses into the rose-garden.

Extensive tree-nurseries are characteristic of the landscape of the district called Pinneberg. Customers from Scandinavia to the Far East, amateur- and landscape-gardeners, fruit farmers as well as forestry engineers and operators of garden centres come to buy their supplies here, and they can choose from as wide a range as 200.000 items.

Baumschule bei Halstenbek / Tree-nursery near Halstenbek

Rosarium in Uetersen / Uetersen, Rosary

Glückstadt: Rathaus / Glückstadt, City Hall

Brockdorff-Palais / Brockdorff-Palace

Mit kühnen politischen Visionen verband der Dänen-könig Christian IV. 1617 die Gründung von **Glück-stadt**. *Der neue Hafen und Handelsplatz, als Festung ausgebaut, sollte Hamburg den Rang ablaufen. Der fächerförmige Grundriss, die herrschaftlichen Adels-palais und Häuserzeilen sind Herzstücke des Stadt-denkmals. Die Zukunft der neuen Stadt lag aber nicht im Handel, sondern in der Verwaltung. Die Glück-städter Kanzlei war Regierungsbehörde bis ins 19. Jahrhundert. Eine wichtige Einnahmequelle war über 200 Jahre die Grönlandfahrt, zu der Dreimaster und Briggs auf Walfang und Robbenjagd ausliefen.*

Im vorigen Jahrhundert machte die Flotte der He-ringslogger im Hafen fest, die im Mai und Juni die an Bord in Fässer eingelegten Heringe aus der Nordsee anlandete. Als Spezialität ist der Ruf des Glückstäd-ter Matjes weit verbreitet – auch wenn er heute aus Norwegen, Dänemark oder Holland kommt.

It was with bold political visions that the Danish king Christian IV in 1617 linked the founding of **Glückstadt**. The new harbour and trading centre – reinforced as a fortress - was supposed to be a challenge to Hamburg. Its fan-like ground-plan, the stately homes and house-fronts are the core-constituents of this urban monu-ment. Yet, the future of the new town did not lie in trade but in the field of administration. Until right into the 19th century Glückstadt's office was the seat of government. For more than 200 years one important source of income was the shipping route to Greenland. Three-masters and brigs sailed north to hunt whales and seals. During the last century the fleet of herring-boats moored in the harbour, and in May and June the herrings were landed that on board had been pickled in barrels. Glückstadt's Matjes-herring is of high re-pute – even if today it is imported from Norway, Denmark, or Holland.

Alter Hafen / Old Port

Krempe und Wilster markierten als Städte den wirtschaftlichen und kulturellen Mittelpunkt in den fruchtbaren Elbmarschen. Von Wohlstand zeugen die Rathäuser, die die Ratsherren im Stil der Renaissance errichten ließen. Sie zählen zu den schönsten baulichen Zeugnissen dieser Epoche. Wenige Kilometer von hier entfernt – in Neuendorf – liegt die tiefste Landstelle Deutschlands: 3,54 m unter dem Meeresspiegel. Mit fünf Atomkraftwerken ist der Unterelberaum ein Zentrum der Kernenergie.

Landeinwärts führt der Weg durch den Kreis Steinburg, mit den ersten karolingischen Burgen und christlichen Taufkirchen nördlich der Elbe. Die Guts-Anlage Breitenburg, unter Heinrich Rantzau Zentrum des Humanismus von europäischem Rang, ist wenige Kilometer von der Kreisstadt Itzehoe entfernt. Im Ständesaal, dem Ort der Holsteinischen Ständeversammlung, liegt eine der Wurzeln des Parlamentarismus in Schleswig-Holstein.

Wilster: Rathaus von 1585 / Wilster, Town-Hall of 1585

Itzehoe: Theater / Itzehoe, Theatre

Krempe and **Wilster** are the economic and cultural centre points in the fertile marshland along the Elbe. The City-Halls in Renaissance style are among the first architectural testimonies to this epoch. Only a few kilometres from here, in **Neuendorf** you can find the lowest land-spot of Germany : 3,54 metres below sea-level . With its five nuclear power plants the area of the lower Elbe is a centre of nuclear energy. Further inland on the route you cross the district of Steinburg with its early Carolingian castles and Christian baptistries north of the Elbe. The manor- house **Breitenburg**, which under Heinrich Rantzau was a centre of Humanism of European status is only a few kilometres away from the district-town **Itzehoe**. The Upper Chamber ('Ständesaal'), site of the Corporative Assembly, is one of the roots of Parliamentarism in Schleswig-Holstein.

Itzehoe: Altes Zentrum mit St. Laurentii
Itzehoe, Old town-centre with St.Laurentii

Itzehoe: Ständehaus – Versammlungs-
ort der Holsteinischen Landstände

Itzehoe, Ständehaus, 'Meeting-place of
body of Holstein representatives

Die Nordsee, Elbe, Eider und der Kanal sind die historischen Grenzen der Landschaft **Ditmarschen**. Sie ist berühmt für ihren Kohl. 80 Millionen Köpfe werden pro Jahr auf dem europaweit größten Anbaugebiet geerntet.

Das Bild der Westküste bestimmen die Generatoren der Windkraftanlagen – markante Zeichen für eine regenerative Energiegewinnung. Wirtschaftlicher Impulsgeber für die Region ist **Brunsbüttel**. Am Endpunkt des Nord-Ostsee-Kanals gelegen, ist die Stadt mit ihrem Elbehafen ein bedeutender Umschlagplatz für Rohstoffe und Massengüter und Mittelpunkt eines großen Industrieareals.

Dithmarscher Bäuerin
Farmer's wife in Dithmarschen

Rapsblüte in Dithmarschen / Flowering rape-field

The North Sea, Elbe, Eider and the Canal are the historical borderlines of the region **Dithmarschen**. It is famous for its cabbage. Up to 80 million heads are picked annually in this biggest cabbage –cultivation area in Europe.

Obvious indication of regenerative energy production are the many high wind power stations. They dominate the scenery on the West Coast. **Brunsbüttel** provides economic impetus for this region. Situated at one end of the Kiel-Canal the town with its harbour on the Elbe has become a major trading post for raw material and bulk goods, and has developed into the centre of a large industrial area.

Bio-Rotkohlernte / Harvesting bio-red-cabbage

Windkraftanlage / Wind-power station

Berühmt ist Dithmarschen auch für die Eigenwilligkeit seiner Bewohner. Erfolgreich im Kampf gegen Flut und Sturm hat sich der reiche freie Bauernstaat gegen jede Obrigkeit behauptet. Am eindrucksvollsten gegen das Söldnerheer ‚Schwarze Garde' der Landesherrn, das bei **Hemmingstedt** geschlagen wurde. Der Schlachtruf „Wahr di, Gaar, de Buur de kummt" aus dem Jahr 1500 ist bis heute lebendiges Erbe.

Die Spuren der Geschichte lassen sich im Landesmuseum in **Meldorf** verfolgen. Im Zentrum steht der Dom, der bedeutendste mittelalterliche Kirchenbau an der Westküste. Er symbolisiert Meldorfs Stellung als geistliches und politisches Zentrum des alten Dithmarschen.
Diese Funktion übernahm die Stadt **Heide**. Auf dem Marktplatz – er ist bis heute der größte in Deutschland – tagte die politische Führung des Bauernstaats. In Heide steht das Geburtshaus des berühmten niederdeutschen Dichters Klaus Groth und in direkter Nachbarschaft das Vaterhaus von Johannes Brahms. Ausstellungen verweisen auf die enge Freundschaft zwischen beiden Künstlern und dokumentieren die norddeutschen Wurzeln des Komponisten.

Meldorfer Mühle
Meldorf, Windmill

Heide: St. Jürgen-Kirche auf dem Marktplatz
Market place with St. Jürgen-church

Blick auf Meldorf
View of Meldorf

However, Dithmarschen is also notorious for the head-strongness of its people.Successful in their struggle against floods and storms, the well-to-do farmers also maintained their position against any form of author-ity. Most impressively this happened against the 'Black Guards', an army of mercenaries that was beaten near Hemmingstedt. Even today their battle cry ' Wahr di, Gaar,de Buur de kummt' – be on your guard, the farm-ers are coming – of 1500 is living heritage.

The central museum in **Meldorf** is an excellent address for studies of local history. In the town's centre, the Cathedral is the major medieval edifice on the West Coast. It symbolizes Meldorf's position as the political and religious centre of historical Dithmarschen. This function was later adopted by **Heide**. The spacious market place, which even in our days is said to be the biggest one in Germany, used to be the site where sat the political establishment of the farming community. In Heide the birthplace of the famous North German poet Klaus Groth can be found in direct neighbour-hood of Johannes Brahms' parental home. Frequent exhibitions give vivid pictures of the close friendship between the two artists and document the North German roots of the celebrated composer of music.

Seehundstation Friedrichskoog
Friedrichskoog, Seal-station

*Gesundes Klima, Ruhe und Natur sind die Merkmale der Küstenregion. In **Friedrichskoog** informiert die Seehundstation über eines der Leittiere des Wattenmeeres. In der Aufnahmestelle für junge Robben, die im Frühsommer verletzt oder verlassen worden sind, werden die „Heuler" betreut und aufgezogen, bis sie im Herbst ausgewildert werden können. Mit **Büsum** hat das Land das älteste Seebad an der Westküste. Gesundheits- und Wellnessangebote locken den Urlauber; und wem der Tag am grünen Deichstrand lang wird, der kann sich in der Erlebniswelt „Blanker Hans" den Naturgewalten der Sturmfluten aussetzen, im Hafen an Bord eines Krabbenfischers gehen oder auf einem Ausflugsschiff Kurs auf Helgoland nehmen.*

Favourable climate, the stillness of nature are characteristics of the coastal region. In **Friedrichskoog** the seal station provides information about one of the most frequent animals of the mud-flats. In a nursing ward for young seals that in early summer were either found injured or were abandoned by their parents, the pups are cared for and raised until in autumn they can again be set free in their natural habitat. **Büsum** is Schleswig-Holstein's oldest seaside resort along the West Coast. Health industries supply for the holiday-makers. For all those who are looking for alternatives to the green grassy beach on the dyke, the theme park 'Blanker Hans' offers opportunities of exposing oneself to the forceful elements of the tides, or else to step on board a crabbing boat – or even to set off for Helgoland on an excursion steamer.

Heuler
Young seal

Alte Kutter im Büsumer Hafen / Old cutters in Büsum harbour

Seebad Büsum / Seaside resort Büsum

Alter Hafen mit den Hütten der Hummerfischer / Old harbour with huts of lobster-fishermen

*Die Felseninsel **Helgoland** mit ihren roten Klippen und der vorgelagerten weißen Düne war Seeräubernest, Schmuggelplatz und deutsch-britisches Tauschobjekt gegen Sansibar. Vorbildlich ist der systematische Wiederaufbau nach der Zerstörung im 2. Weltkrieg und der Rückkehr der Bewohner 1952. Mit der „Biologischen Anstalt" und der „Vogelwarte" haben hier international renommierte Forschungseinrichtungen ihren Sitz. Das wintermilde Klima und die vielen Sonnenstunden machen die Insel, auf der Hoffmann von Fallersleben den Text zum Deutschlandlied schrieb, zu einer Hochburg für Touristen. Die Bäderschiffe liegen auf Reede vor Anker, die Gäste werden aus- und eingebootet. Eine Besonderheit ist der Lummenfels, von dem sich im Sommer die Küken der Hochseevögel auf den Ruf der Alten ins Meer stürzen.*

The rocky island **Helgoland** with its red cliffs and white offshore dune used to be a hideout for pirates, for smugglers and was also German-British exchange object for Sansibar. The systematic post-war reconstruction and the return of the island's residents in 1952 are exemplary. Prestigious international research institutes have their headquarters here. Both the Biological- and the Ornithological Institute ('Biologische Anstalt' and 'Vogelwarte') may serve as examples here. The mild climate in wintertime and many guaranteed hours of sunshine in summer have turned the island, on which Hugo von Hofmannsthal wrote the lyrics for Germany's national anthem, into a favourite destination for holidaymakers. Ships are lying in the roads and the passengers are regularly being embarked or disembarked. Of special interest is the 'Lummenfels', where in summer the birds' chicks that cannot yet fly, plunge from the rock into the sea at the command of their parents.

Börteboot / Embarking passengers

Lummenkolonie / Colony of guillemots

Felsen „Lange Anna" / Long Anna, Famous rock

Wie der Dänenkönig Christian, so träumte auch der Gottorfer Herzog Friedrich III. von einem Welthandelshafen, als er 1621 am Zusammenfluss von Treene und Eider eine Stadt gründete. Holländische Glaubensflüchtlinge wurden als Siedler geworben und legten **Friedrichstadt** nach heimischen Vorbildern an. Das Versprechen der Religionsfreiheit zog neben den Remonstranten portugiesische Juden, Protestanten, Katholiken, Quäker und Mennoniten an. Vier Gotteshäuser bekunden bis heute die Konfessionsvielfalt. Die Holländerstadt mit ihren Grachten und Sielzügen, den Brücken und hohen Treppengiebelhäusern gilt als „Venedig des Nordens".

Like the Danish King Christian, so did the Duke of Gottorf Friedrich III dream of an international trading port when in 1621 he laid the foundation - stone of a town at the confluence of the rivers Trave and Eider.

Am historischen Brunnen / Historical fountain

Refugees from Holland who had left their country for religious reasons were won as settlers. They planned and built **Friedrichstadt** along their own familiar models. Apart from the Dutch 'Remonstrants', the promise of religious freedom also attracted Portuguese Jews, Protestants, Catholics, Quakers and Mennonites. Even today four churches tell of this variety of religious denominations. The Dutch town with its canals, weirs, bridges, and gabled roof houses is considered the 'Venice of the North'.

Grachtenfahrt / Boat trip on a canal

Häuserzeile am Markt / Market place with row of houses

Tönning: Kirchturm
Tönning, Church tower

Packhaus / Storehouse

An der Eidermündung gelegen, war die Stadt und Festung **Tönning** der wichtigste Ausfuhrhafen für die Produkte der Halbinsel Eiderstedt: Weizen, Wolle, Fleisch, Käse, aber auch Rinder und Schafe wurden von hier aus verschifft. Das repräsentative Packhaus gibt einen Eindruck vom Volumen der gelagerten Waren. Das Stadtbild prägt der hohe Barockhelm auf dem Turm der Kirche, in der ein Epitaph mit dem Selbstbildnis des in Tönning geborenen Barock-Malers Jürgen Ovens zu finden ist.

Situated at the mouth of the river Eider the town and fortress called **Tönning** was the most important port of exit for the goods produced here on the peninsula Eiderstedt. Wheat, wool, meat, cheese, but also livestock like cattle and sheep were shipped from here. The impressive 'Packhaus' is indicative of the range and volume of the goods stored here. The spire of the church is a distinct feature of the town. Within an epitaph with a self-portrait of Tönning-born Jürgen Ovens, painter of the Baroque period, can be seen.

Hafen bei Ebbe / Harbour at ebb-tide

Sperrwerk mit geöffneten Fluttoren / Eider Damm with opened flood gates

Ein technisches Meisterwerk haben Ingenieure mit dem **Eidersperrwerk** *geschaffen, das die Region gegen die Sturmfluten der Nordsee schützt und zugleich für eine Binnenentwässerung sorgt. Die 200 Meter breite Anlage mit fünf Fluttoren, die bei Gefahr geschlossen werden, und die angegliederte Schleuse für den Schiffsverkehr sind ein Magnet für Besucher.*

The brilliant engineers who designed and constructed the **Eidersperrwerk** (Eider Dam) created a technical masterpiece that has since protected the region against the storm tides and has at the same time ensured inland drainage. Both the 200-metres-wide construction with its five flood gates, which in cases of emergency can be shut, and the shipping lock right next to it regularly attract great numbers of visitors.

Multimar Wattforum in Tönning

*Die Halbinsel Eiderstedt ist das Kernstück des Nationalparks Schleswig-Holsteinisches Wattenmeer, eines der größten europäischen Schutzgebiete. In den Aquarien und dem Walhaus des **Multimar Wattforums** wird die Vielfalt dieses Naturraums in ökologischen Zusammenhängen aufgezeigt. Watt, Salzwiese, Düne, Strand und Meer sollen im Einklang mit der wirtschaftlichen Nutzung geschützt werden, ebenso wie die Gebiete, in denen seltene Vogelarten heimisch sind und Zugvögel Station machen.*

The peninsula Eiderstedt is the core of the National Park Schleswig-Holsteinisches Wattenmeer (National Park of the Wadden Sea), one of the major European nature reserves. In the aquariums and the whalehouse of the **Multimar Wattforum** the great diversity of this largely untouched region is displayed in ecological contexts and made available for the public to see. Tideland, salt marshes, dunes, beaches, and the sea are being protected in accord with economic utilization, as are areas where rare indigenous species of birds are living or where migratory birds stop off on their way.

Strand von St.Peter-Ording / Beach at St.Peter-Ording

Kitesurfer / Kite surfer

*Seit mehr als 125 Jahren ist **St. Peter-Ording** das Ziel von Gästen, die im Reizklima Erholung suchen. Die Seebrücke, der Strand mit den Pfahlbauten und die Sandbank markieren das Sport-Revier: Gymnastik, Beachvolleyball, Kitesurfen, Strandsegeln und jeder neue Trend sind angesagt. Strandläufer können mit Glück auch heute noch ein Stück Bernstein finden.*

For more than 125 years now **St.Peter Ording** has been the destination of visitors looking for relaxation in the stimulating climate there. The long sea-bridge, the beach with its stilt houses, and the huge sandbank provide ample facilities for recreation: gymnastics, beach volleyball, kite-surfing, sand-yachting – any new trend is taken up here. Strollers along the beach may well be lucky to find a piece of amber there right at their feet.

Leuchtturm Westerhever
Lighthouse Westerhever

Roter Haubarg / Elaborate farmhouse

Kirche von Westerhever / Westerhever, Church

Hoyersworth

*Die Fahrt nach **Westerhever** mit dem Fußmarsch durch die Salzwiesen zum Leuchtturm ist Pflichtprogramm, nicht nur für Fotografen. Er ist ein Wahrzeichen für die Halbinsel **Eiderstedt** wie die prachtvoll ausgestatteten historischen Kirchen, von denen 18 erhalten sind, und die Haubarge. Diese Großbauernhöfe – beispielhaft der Hochdorfer Haubarg in Tating oder der Rote Haubarg in Witzwort – sind Zeugnisse des einst reichen Bauernlandes.*

The trip to **Westerhever** and the walk across the salt meadows to the lighthouse is a must not only for photographers. It is a landmark on the peninsula, as are the 18 splendid historical churches that have remained in good condition, and the elaborate farm houses (Haubarge). The Hochdorfer Haubarg in Tating and the Red Haubarg in Witzwort are notable examples of the people's affluence in this area.

Polderlandschaft bei Kating / Polder-area near Kating

Haubarg bei Westerhever / Haubarg near Westerhever

Hafen / Harbour

Stormhaus / Storm's house

Tine

Marktkirche mit Tine-Brunnen
Church with Tine-fountain

Als „graue Stadt am Meer" hat Theodor Storm seine Geburtsstadt **Husum** weltweit bekannt gemacht. Als der wichtigste Platz für den Kornhandel mit den Niederlanden war die gottorfische Hafenstadt das Tor zum Westen. Heute ist Husum das Tor zur Halligwelt. Touristen machen am Binnenhafen, dem Marktplatz mit der von C.F. Hansen erbauten klassizistischen Kirche und dem Tine-Brunnen Station, besuchen das Storm-Haus und flanieren im Frühjahr durch den mit Krokusblüten übersäten Garten des von Herzog Adolf erbauten Renaissance-Schlosses.

Schloss: Torhaus / Gatehouse

Theodor Storm made his native town **Husum** famous worldwide be referring to it as 'the grey town by the sea'. As the most important place for the corn trade with the Netherlands, this Gottorf sea-port was the gateway to the west. Today it is the gateway to the world of the Halligen ,small islets off the coast of Schleswig-Holstein. Tourists stop over at the harbour, the market-place with the classical church, built by C.F.Hansen, and the Tine-Fountain.They visit Storm's birthplace – and in spring may relax in the garden of the Renaissance castle, built by Duke Adolf, with its flowering crocusses.

Husumer Krokusblütenkönigin
'queen of crocuses'

Schloss / Castle

Hooge: Priellandschaft / Hooge, Narrow channel-landscape

Ebbe und Flut bestimmen den Alltag auf den **Halligen** vor der nordfriesischen Küste, Sturmfluten bedrohen im Frühjahr und Herbst Mensch und Vieh. Bei „Landunter" ragen allein die meterhoch aufgeschütteten Warften aus dem Meer. Nur die Hälfte der zehn deutschen Halligen ist bewirtschaftet. Die Bewohner leben von der Viehwirtschaft und von den Ausflüglern, die es auf der Fahrt über das Wattenmeer zu den Seehundbänken vor allem nach **Hooge** zieht. Auf den kleinen, unbewohnten Halligen nimmt nur der Vogelschützer Quartier.

Kirchwarft / Promontory with church

Hooge: Königspesel
Hooge, Main room of house, in which the King stayed

High and low tide determine the daily routine on the **Halligen**. In spring and autumn storm tides endanger both man and beast. In cases of 'land under water' only the tiny promontories thrown up meters high remain visible. Of the ten German Halligen only half are being farmed. The people who have made their home there earn their living by raising cattle or by catering for visitors who are on their way across the mudflats past the seal-banks towards the islet **Hooge**, the area's main attraction. The small uninhabited Halligen on the other hand are only used by bird conservationists.

Seehund-Sandbank / Sandbank with seals

Das Meer gibt, das Meer nimmt: Inseln sind entstanden und untergegangen. Wie das Kirchspiel Rungholt, das in der ‚Groten Mandränke' vom Januar 1362 versank. Bis heute lebt die Legende von der reichen Stadt, deren Glocken bei ruhigem Wetter unter der Wasseroberfläche zu hören sein sollen: unangefochten von archäologischen Forschungsergebnissen.

The sea gives, the sea takes away again – islands were born and later disappeared again. Just like the parish Rungholt which disappeared in 1362 in the 'Groten Mandränke'. The legend of the rich town whose churchbells are said to be audible under the water-surface in calm weather has been handed down to this day – undisputed even by archaeological research.

Fahrwassermarkierungen / Shipping channel, maritime signals

Gezeitenformen / Tidal traces

Fußspuren / Footprints

Klaffmuschel / Soft shell clam

Strandgut / Flotsam and jetsam

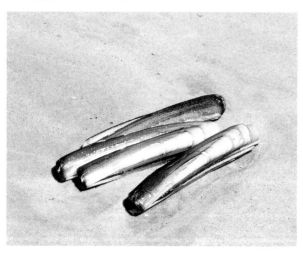

Seeregenpfeifer / Sea-plover

Austernfischer / Oyster catcher

Krabbenkutter im Wattenmeer / Shrimp cutter in the mud-flats

Kniepsand

*Mit einem der breitesten Sandstrände Nordeuropas profiliert sich **Amrum** unter den drei großen Nordfriesischen Inseln. Dabei ist der Kniepsand eine wandernde Sandbank des Meeres. Die Windmühlen erinnern an Zeiten, in denen Landwirtschaft, Fischfang und Seefahrt die Bewohner ernährt haben, bevor die Badegäste das Geld brachten. Für sie wurde 1890 **Wittdün** am Fährhafen gegründet. Das Festland erreicht man per Schiff, die Nachbarinsel Föhr in zwei bis drei Stunden zu Fuß – vorausgesetzt, es ist Niedrigwasser.*

Of the three North Frisian islands **Amrum** boasts one of the broadest sandy beaches in northern Europe. The 'Kniepsand' is a constantly shifting sanddune. Windmills tell of times past when agriculture, fishing industry and maritime trade fed the inhabitants before later on tourism took over and became the main source of income. It was for the tourists that in 1890 Wittdün at the ferry terminal was founded. It takes the boat to get to the mainland, the neighbouring island Föhr, however, can be reached on foot within two or three hours – provided there is low tide.

Kapitänshaus in Nebel / Captains's house in Nebel

Leuchtturm / Lighthouse

Auf der „grünen Insel" **Föhr** mit Bauerngärten und alten Bäumen wird gut Zweidrittel der Fläche landwirtschaftlich genutzt. **Wyk** ist das erste Nordseebad der Herzogtümer, das im Gründungsjahr 1819 gerade 61 Gäste verzeichnete. Spuren der Vergangenheit lassen sich an der Lembecksburg, den mittelalterlichen Kirchen und den Grabsteinen ablesen, die von Seefahrern und Walfängern berichten. Inselgeschichte erzählt auch das Museum in Wyk. Viele Bräuche sind lebendig. Zu dem aus heidnischer Zeit stammenden Bikebrennen, mit dem am 21. Februar die Walfänger aus ihrer Heimat verabschiedet wurden, lodern Feuer aus Reisighaufen auf allen Inseln und Halligen, aber auch an der Küste. Die gemeinsame Geschichte in reichen wie in kargen Zeiten, in denen Familien nach Amerika auswanderten, Brauchtum und die friesische Sprache sind das innere Band Nordfrieslands.

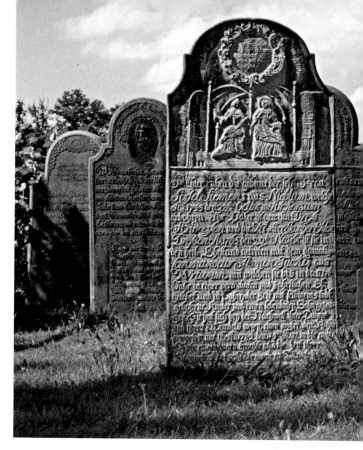

Nieblum: Friedhof / Nieblum, Graveyard

On the 'green island' **Föhr** with its farmhouse gardens and veteran trees more than two thirds of the area are used for agriculture. **Wyk** was the first North Sea seaside-resort of the duchies. In the year of its foundation,1819, it just hosted 61 guests. Traces of the past can be detected at the 'Lembecksburg', the medieval churches and the tombstones that tell of seafaring and whaling. The island's history is also shown in Wyk's museum. Many of the old customs and traditions have survived, like for instance the pagan 'Bikebrennen': in times past on February 21 the whaling boats were seen off by lighting huge fires. Even today fires are set not only on all the islands and Halligen, but also on the mainland along the coastal line. A mutual history in good times as well as in those bad days when families emigrated to America, also shared customs and traditions, and the Frisian language – all these togeher constitute the close tie that can be felt everywhere in North Friesland.

Strandpromenade von Wyk
Wyk, Promenade

Westerland-Promenade

Es hält auch die Insel **Sylt**, beliebt wegen ihrer Landschaft zwischen Strand und Watt, berühmt wegen der Promis, die Kampen als Szene-Treff populär machten. Viele kleine Gemeinden konnten ihren Charakter gegen den Tourismusboom erhalten; so wie Keitum, einer der ältesten Inselorte, mit den Häusern der reichen Walfänger und der St. Severin Kirche, dem kirchlichen und kulturellen Mittelpunkt der Insel. Mitte des 19. Jahrhunderts wurde Westerland das ständig wachsende Versorgungszentrum. Zwischen den Häfen Hörnum und List liegen geschützte Naturräume: das Ratumbecken, die Vogelkoje, das Rote Kliff, die Braderuper Heide, die Wanderdünen in Listland und der Ellenbogen mit dem nördlichsten Landpunkt Deutschlands. Es liegen aber auch 40 km Küste mit einem breiten Sandstrand zwischen Nord- und Südspitze, die Jahr für Jahr mit aufwendigen Sandvorspülungen vor dem Abtrag durch die Sturmfluten geschützt werden müssen. Von List startet die Syltfähre zur dänischen Nachbarinsel Rømø. Auf der Strecke Niebüll-Westerland rollen Personen- und Autozüge über den 1927 eröffneten Hindenburgdamm vom Festland auf die Insel.

Rotes Kliff / Red Clif

This also applies to **Sylt**, an island popular for its outstanding beauty between beach and mudflats, famous for its prominent people who have made Kampen the centre of the hip-scene. A good number of small communities succeeded in retaining their respective character against the onslaught of tourism. Like, for instance, Keitum, one of the oldest places on the island, with its houses of former well-to-do whalers and the church of St.Severin, the religious and cultural focus on the island. In the middle of the 19th century Westerland became the steadily growing supply-centre. Between the harbours of Hörnum and List protected unspoilt countryside can be found everywhere: the Rantum basin, the 'Vogelkoje', the Red Cliff, Braderup Heathland, the shifting sanddunes near List and the 'Elbow' which is the northernmost point on land in Germany. Between the north and the southernmost point,however, there are 40 kilometres of sandy coastal line which every year must be protected against the high tides by depositing loads of new sand on the offshore breakwaters. The ferry to the neighbouring Danish island Rømø leaves from here. On the route from Westerland to Niebüll passenger- and motorail-trains have since 1927 rolled over the Hindenburg Causeway that links Sylt with the mainland.

Rotes Kliff

Kirche St. Severin / Church of St.Severin

Keitum: Friesenhaus / Keitum, Frisian house

Heidelerche / Lark

Wanderdüne / Drifting sand dune

Heide- und Dünenlandschaft / Heathland and sand-dunes

Bildersaal / Picture hall

Nolde: Selbstbildnis / Self-portrait

In **Seebüll**, nahe der dänischen Grenze, hat Emil Nolde 1930 das von ihm entworfene Wohnhaus mit Atelier bezogen, in dem er 1956 starb. Im heutigen Museum wird das Werk des Künstlers gezeigt, der zu den bedeutendsten Malern des Expressionismus gehört: mit seinen religiösen Bildern, den Grafiken, den Gemälden, den „ungemalten Bildern" aus der Zeit des Nationalsozialismus, in der er als „entartet" galt, und den leuchtenden Blumenaquarellen. Sie entstanden in dem Garten, der in jedem Jahr wie zu Noldes Zeiten farbenprächtig erblüht.

In **Seebüll**, near the border to Denmark, Emil Nolde lived in the house and studio designed by himself in 1930. He also died there in 1957. In the museum today the oeuvre that made him one of the most outstanding painters of Expressionism is displayed to the public. There are his religious pictures, his graphic art and magnificent paintings, and also the 'unpainted pictures' from Nazi times, when his art was branded 'degenerate'. His flower watercolours were painted here in the garden which every year boasts a glorious sea of blossoms – just like in Nolde's own days.

Wohn- und Atelierhaus / Residential building and studio

Die nördlichste Stadt der Bundesrepublik liegt unmittelbar an der Grenze zu Dänemark. Über 400 Jahre gehörte **Flensburg** mit der Region zur dänischen Krone und war zeitweise die bedeutendste Handelsstadt des Nordens. Ihre Kaufleute hielten Kontakte zu den Ostseehäfen, nach Norwegen, Frankreich und Spanien und schalteten sich in den atlantischen Dreieckshandel zwischen Europa, Afrika und Amerika ein. Rum war das Produkt, das das Image der Stadt bis heute prägt. Nach dem 1. Weltkrieg wurde die Grenze im Norden neu gezogen: per Volksabstimmung kam Nordschleswig zu Dänemark, Flensburg wurde Grenzstadt. Nachhaltige Spannungen zwischen den nationalen Minderheiten konnten durch die Bonn-Kopenhagener Erklärungen entschärft werden, die Wege des friedlichen Zusammenlebens aufzeigten. Sie gelten als Modell für das zusammenwachsende Europa. Flensburg ist der Sitz der dänischen Minderheit, hier weht der Danebrog im Stadtbild. Zwischen Südermarkt und Nordertor in der historischen Altstadt liegen die mittelalterlichen Kirchen St. Marien und St. Nikolai, Wohnhäuser, Spei-

cher und Kaufmannshöfe mit Restaurants, Boutiquen, Handwerksbetrieben und Galerien. Flensburg ist berüchtigt wegen der Verkehrssünderkartei beim Kraftfahrtbundesamt, angesehen als Handballhochburg und populär durch die Biermarke „Flens" und den Beate Uhse Erotik-Versand. Es ist Wirtschafts- und Kulturzentrum, Hochschulstandort, Marinestützpunkt mit der Marineschule Mürwik und eine Fördestadt, die vor dem deutsch-dänischen Ufer eines der schönsten Segelreviere aufweisen kann. Eine weltweit bekannte Adresse unter den vielen Segelclubs ist die Hanseatische Yachtschule im Seebad **Glücksburg**.

The northernmost town of the Federal Republic is situated directly at the borderline to Denmark . For more than 400 years **Flensburg** and its surrounding region belonged to the Danish crown, and for some time it was the major centre of commerce in the north. Businessmen kept close contact with Norway, with the trading ports along the Baltic coast, with France and Spain, and also joined in with the Atlantic three-way-

Nordermarkt mit Marienkirche / Nordermarkt with Church of St.Mary

Letztes seegängiges Kohle befeuertes
Passagierdampfschiff

Last sea-going coal fuelled passenger steamer

ALEXANDRA

Speicher / Storehouse

Rumhaus Johannsen/Rum-house

Nordertor / Gate to the North

Schiffbrückstraße mit „Windsbraut"

Große Straße / Shopping mall

Rote Straße: Hof / Courtyard

deal between Europe, Africa, and America. Since then rum has been the product that determined the image of the town. After World War I the borderline in the north was newly drawn: by referendum North-Schleswig was assigned to Denmark, and Flensburg thus became border town. Lingering tensions between the respective minorities were eased by the Bonn-Copenhagen Declarations, which pointed out ways for peaceful coexistence, and which have since become a model for the merging of Europe. Flensburg is the headquarters of the Danish minority, the 'Danebrog' (Danish flag) is omnipresent in the town. Between 'Südermarkt' and 'Nordertor' are the medieval churches of St.Mary and St. Nikolai, also residential buildings,

silos and former retailers' backyards that today have been turned into cozy restaurants, boutiques, galleries, and workshops. Apart from all that Flensburg is notorious for its central index of traffic offenders at the Federal Agency for Motorvehicles, it has a superb reputation as a stronghold of handball, and is popular due to its local beer ('Flens') and Beate Uhse's mail order company for erotica. It is an economic and cultural centre, university town, naval base with its Naval Academy Mürwik and it is a fjord-town that may well boast one of the most beautiful yachting areas. An internationally accredited address among the many sailing clubs is the Hanseatic Yachting School in the seaside resort **Glücksburg**.

Das weithin sichtbare Wasserschloss **Glücksburg** mit den vier Ecktürmen ist einer der schönsten Renaissancebauten des Landes. Auf dem Gelände des ehemaligen Klosters Rude errichtet, war es Sitz der Glücksburger Herzöge und Sommerresidenz des dänischen Königs. Über Christian IX. ist die Glücksburger Linie mit den Königshäusern von Schweden, England, Russland, Griechenland und Norwegen verwandt. Das Schloss ist als Museum und Veranstaltungsort ein kulturelles Zentrum mit überregionaler Anziehungskraft.

Visible from far away is the **Glücksburg** Castle in the Lake with its four corner towers. It is one of the finest Renaissance edifices in Schleswig-Holstein. Built upon the site of the former monastery Rude,it was the seat of the Dukes of Glücksburg and summer residence of the Danish King. Christian IX is the connecting link of the Glücksburg-line with the royal dynasties of Sweden, England, Russia, Greece, and Norway. As a museum and a place for public events, the castle now has become a cultural centre with more than just regional appeal and significance.

Heringszaun / Herring-fence

*Von der Flensburger Förde bis zur Schlei erstreckt sich die Landschaft Angeln, deren Bewohner im 5. Jahrhundert mit Sachsen und Jüten Britannien eroberten. Die idyllische Region mit Kirchen aus kunstvoll behauenen Granitquadern ist ein beliebter Drehort und Ziel für Touristen. Daran knüpft die Stadt **Kappeln** mit den jährlichen Heringstagen an. Die Fische, die zum Laichen von der Ostsee in die Schlei schwimmen, verfangen sich im Heringszaun. 500 Jahre ist er alt und die einzig erhaltene von ehemals 38 Anlagen. Ein Kulturdenkmal wie die Windmühle Amanda und St. Nicolai, der letzte bedeutende Kirchenbau des Spätbarock im Lande.*

The countryside of Angeln stretches from Flensburg's fjord to the Schlei. Together with Saxons and Jutes its inhabitants took part in the conquest of Britain in the 5th century. The idyllic region with its churches built of skilfully hewn granite ashlars is a favourite location and destination for tourists. The town of **Kappeln**, for instance, offers its annual herring days, a popular attraction. The fish that migrate from the Baltic into the Schlei in search of their spawning grounds get caught in the herring fence. Of the 38 former such fences the one left over is 500 years old and is the last of its kind. It is a cultural monument, as are the windmill Amanda and St. Nikolai, the last important church of the late Baroque in Schleswig-Holstein.

Kappeln

Rittersaal / Knights' Hall Hauptportal / Main portal Globus / Globe

Am Ufer der Schlei prägt der Dom die Silhouette der Stadt **Schleswig**. Zu seiner prächtigen Ausstattung gehört der aus der Klosterkirche Bordesholm stammende Altar von Hans Brüggemann – ein Hauptwerk mittelalterlicher Holzschnitzkunst. Ein besonderer

Teil der Altstadt sind das Kloster St. Johannis und die Fischersiedlung **Holm**. Die Bewohner leben in kleinen Giebelhäusern um den Friedhof herum; in der Gemeinschaft ist die Gilde-Tradition lebendig. Schleswig wurde nach dem Untergang Haithabus für 200

Schloss Gottorf / Gottorf Castle

Globushaus und Barock-Garten / Globe house and baroque garden

Jahre Drehscheibe im nordeuropäischen Fernhandel. Die Stadt war Mittelpunkt des Herzogtums, Regierungssitz der preußischen Provinz und bekam, als nach dem Kriegsende Kiel Hauptstadt wurde, die Obergerichte des Landes, das Landesarchiv und die Landesmuseen. Sie sind im **Schloss Gottorf** *eingerichtet worden. Das hatte seine Glanzzeit als Residenz der Gottorfer Landesfürsten. Der repräsentative Hof galt mit der Bibliothek und der Kunstkammer europaweit als Zentrum für Wissenschaft und Kunst, an dem der Universalgelehrte Adam Olearius und der Barockmaler Jürgen Ovens wirkten. Mit der Rekonstruktion des Barockgartens und des Riesenglobus wird im Ensemble die frühere Ausstrahlung dieses Ortes wieder erkennbar.*

High above the Schlei the spire of the **Schleswig** Cathedral gives the landscape its character. The altar carved by Hans Brüggemann – which originally belongs to the monastery in Bordesholm – is one of the principal works of medieval wood carving. Of individual interest in the old part of town are the monastery St. Johannis and the fishing village **Holm**. The small gabled houses are arranged around the cemetery with its chapel. Families still maintain the tradition of the old guilds. For 200 years after the decline of Haithabu, Schleswig not only gained the pivotal role in North-European international trade, but also became the centre of the duchy, seat of government of the Prussian province, and eventually, when after the end of the war Kiel was made capital, Schleswig became the home of Schleswig-Holstein's main courts of law. Also the central museums and the state's archives were transferred to Schleswig and found their respective homes in **'Schloss Gottorf'**, the local castle. This building had its heyday as residence of the Gottorf sovereign princes. All over Europe its impressive courtyard, together with the library and the chamber of art was considered a centre of science and art, where, for instance, Adam Olearius, the universal genius and the Baroque painter Jürgen Ovens worked. After the reconstruction of the Baroque garden and the giant globe the former attraction of this place has again become perceptible.

Holm

Kloster St.Johannis / Convent

Dom / Cathedral

Brüggemann-Altar

Haithabu: Museum am alten Siedlungsort / Haithabu, Museum at the site of the ancient settlement

Ausstellung / Exhibition

Nachbauten der Wikingerhäuser / Replicas of Viking houses

*Auf dem anderen Ufer der Schlei liegt **Haithabu**. Die durch das Danewerk und einen Halbkreiswall geschützte Wikingersiedlung war von 800 bis zur Zerstörung 1066 der wichtigste Handelsplatz Nordeuropas. Die Archäologischen Forschungen an dieser Stätte bringen grundlegende Einsichten in den Prozess der Stadtentstehung. Sie sind im Wikinger-Museum dargestellt, dessen Hauptattraktion das aus dem Haddebyer Noor geborgene Langschiff ist.*

Haithabu is situated on the other bank of the Schlei. From 800 to its destruction in 1066 this Viking settlement, protected by the 'Danewerk' and a semi-circle wall was the most important trading place of northern Europe. Archaeological research has provided insights into the settlement's earliest history. Findings are on display in the Viking Museum with its main attraction, the longboat, found in the Haddebyer Noor. Today replicas of medieval dwellings are added and bring renewed interest to the area.

Gut Ludwigsburg / Estate Ludwigsburg

*Die Halbinsel Schwansen zwischen Schlei und Ek-
kernförder Bucht ist eine historische Gutslandschaft.
Zu ihr gehört das denkmalgeschützte Dorf **Sieseby**.
An der Küste ist in **Damp** ein modernes Zentrum für
Gesundheit und Wellness entstanden.*

The peninsula Schwansen set between the Schlei and
the Eckernförde fjord is an historical area of land-
owners and their property. **Sieseby**, the listed village, is
typical of this region. At the coast **Damp** has grown
into a modern rehabilitation- and wellness-centre.

Sieseby: Dorfstraße / Sieseby, Village street

Zentrum Damp / Damp Center

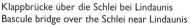

Klappbrücke über die Schlei bei Lindaunis
Bascule bridge over the Schlei near Lindaunis

Damp: Wellnessbereich / Wellness area

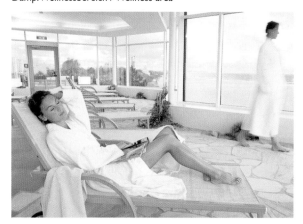

Eckernförde: Hafen / Eckernförde, Harbour

Räucherfisch / Smoking fish

*Nur wenige Kilometer südlich liegt das Ostseebad **Eckernförde**. In dem früheren Fischerort wird bis heute die „Kieler Sprotte" geräuchert. Im Hafen machen im Sommer Traditionsschiffe und Segelboote fest. Touristen zieht es über die Nikolaikirche und den Markt mit dem Alten Rathaus durch die Einkaufsstraße oder die engen Gassen an den Strand. Auf dem Gelände der ehemaligen Torpedoversuchsanstalt ist die Erprobungsstelle für Schiffe und Marinewaffen der Bundeswehr.*

Only a few kilometres to the south you reach **Eckernförde**, the seaside resort on the Baltic coast. From historical times, when it was a small fishing village, the tradition of smoking 'Kieler Sprotten' (Kiel sprats) has been handed down into our days. In the summer veteran ships and modern sailing craft are moored in the harbour along the wooden bridge. Tourists make their way across the historical centre with its market-place, the old Town Hall and the church of St.Nikolai, its pedestrian shopping precincts or the narrow lanes towards the beach. On the terrain of the former testing plant for torpedoes one can now find the test range for ships and naval weapons of the Federal Navy .

Markt mit Nikolaikirche / Market with church

Kieler Hafen / Kiel harbour

Norwegenterminal
Norway-terminal

Am sturmsicheren Fördehafen gründete der Schau-enburger Graf Adolf IV. **Kiel** als Stützpunkt im Ost-seehandel. Als Sitz der Universität wurde die Mittelstadt das geistige und kulturelle Zentrum der Herzogtümer und zeitweilig Hauptresidenz der Hol-stein-Gottorfer Herzöge. Die entscheidende Zäsur brachte die Einverleibung der Herzogtümer in Preu-ßen, die vom Kieler Schloss proklamiert wurde: 1871 wurde Kiel Reichskriegshafen. Die Werften und die Zulieferindustrie boomten, die Bevölkerung wuchs, neue Wohnviertel entstanden. Kaiser Wilhelm II. ver-lieh der Stadt Glanz – durch seine Teilnahme an der Kieler Woche und der Eröffnung des Nord-Ostsee-Kanals. Kiel lebte mit der Marine und durch die Ma-rine. Hier wurden mit dem Matrosenaufstand im November 1918 die Weichen vom Kaiserreich zur Re-publik gestellt.

Nach dem 2. Weltkrieg wurde Kiel Hauptstadt des Bundeslandes Schleswig-Holstein. Der Landtag be-zog das „Haus an der Förde", die ehemalige Marine-akademie.

Der Wiederaufbau der im Bombenhagel zerstörten Stadt setzte auf die alten Ressourcen. Die Werftin-dustrie ist bis heute mit dem Maschinenbau ein wichtiger Wirtschaftsfaktor, der Hafen positioniert sich als Knotenpunkt für den Fährverkehr und die Schiffe der Kreuzfahrer. Meereskunde ist ein For-schungsschwerpunkt der Universität. Die land-schaftlich reizvolle Lage prägt den Charakter der Stadt, die Verknüpfung von Wirtschaft, Wissen-schaft, Kultur und Sport bestimmt ihre Perspektiven.

The Schauenburger Duke Adolf IV founded Kiel as a Baltic trading-stronghold along the sheltered harbour. The existence of the university made the medium-sized city the intellectual centre of the dukedoms. Temporarily the castle was the main residence of the Dukes of Holstein-Gottorf. The decisive caesura came with the incorporation of the dukedoms into Prussia, proclaimed from Kiel Castle. In 1871 Kiel became 'Reichskriegshafen' (Naval Port of the Reich).

Shipbuilding and ancillary industries grew rapidly, the population increased, new residential areas came into being. Due to the Emperor Wilhelm II's participation in the Kiel Week and the opening of the Kiel Canal, new splendour was added to the city. Kiel lived with the Navy and profited from the Navy. Here – in November 1918 – the revolt of the sailors started the revolution that opened the way from imperial rule to republic-anism.

Soon after World War II, Kiel became the capital of the Federal State Schleswig-Holstein. Its parliament moved into the 'House on the Fjord', formerly Marine Academy. Reconstruction of the city that had almost completely been destroyed in the air-raids, relied on its traditional resources. Until today shipbuilding in-dustries together with mechanical engineering have been important economic factors. The harbour in Kiel is positioning itself as a junction for ferry traffic as well as for impressive cruise ships. Oceanography is a main target of research at the university.

It is its attractive scenic location that shapes the city's character, and the combination of industry and com-merce with science, culture, and sports determines its perspectives.

Portalkräne der Howaldtswerke / HDW's portal cranes

Hörnbrücke / Bridge across the Hörn

Kiellinie: Spaß für Jung und Alt / Fun equally for old and young

Segelschulschiff 'Gorch Fock' am Marinehafen
The training sailing ship at the naval port

Saison an den Kais / High season at the quays

Super-Kreuzfahrtfähre auf der Route Kiel Oslo
Super cruise ferry Kiel-Oslo

Ruhezone Bootshafen / Recreational area

*Rathaus und Opernhaus bilden am Kleinen Kiel
ein zweites Zentrum.*

*City Hall and Opera House, both situated
alongside the 'Kleiner Kiel', are forming a second centre.*

Hörncampus

Ostseehalle

Ernst Barlachs „Geistkämpfer": 1928 als Mahnmal vor der Heiliggeist-Kirche aufgestellt; 1936 entfernt; 1954 vor der Nikolaikirche wieder errichtet.

Ernst Barlach, 'Geistkämpfer', Erected 1928 in front of the Holy-Ghost-Church as a memorial; removed 1936; re-erected 1954 in front of the Nikolai-Church

In der historischen Altstadt sind der Kreuzgang des Heiliggeist-Klosters, die Nikolaikirche, das Stadtmuseum Warleberger Hof, der Rantzaubau und die Fischhalle Zeugnisse des alten Kiel. Um den Schlossgarten war und ist mit der Kunsthalle, den Museen, dem Konzertsaal und der Landesbibliothek der kulturelle Mittelpunkt.

In the historical part of the city, the cross course of the 'Heiliggeist-Kloster', 'Nikolai-Kirche', the city museum 'Warleberger Hof', the 'Rantzau Building' and the 'Fischhalle' provide a vivid picture of what the city looked like. Set around the 'Schlossgarten' (Castle garden), the 'Kunsthalle' (Art Gallery), the museums, the Concert Hall and the region's library constitute the cultural centre of the city.

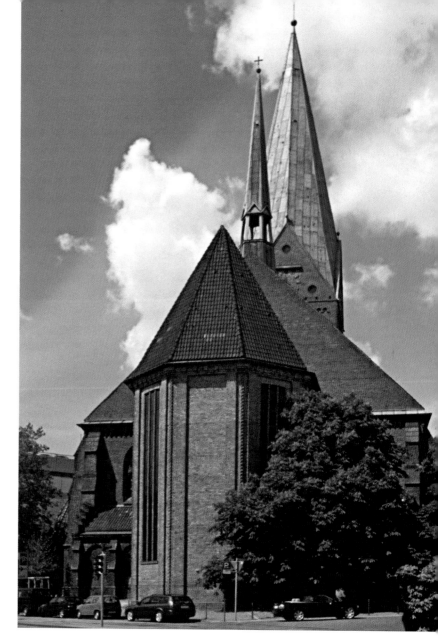

Nikolaikirche / Nikolai-Church

Schiffahrtsmuseum in der ehemaligen Fischhalle
Shipping Museum in the former Fishmarket Hall

Kieler Woche: Hansekogge mit Gaffelseglern / Kiel-Week, Hanseatic cog and gaffsail boats

Als Mekka des Segelsports mit dem internationalen Höhepunkt der Kieler Woche pflegt die Stadt das Image der „sailing city". Das Marine-Ehrenmal in Laboe, das Olympiazentrum in Schilksee, die Schleusen am Nord-Ostseekanal sind Anziehungspunkte für Besucher und Einheimische: wie Kiellinie und Hindenburgufer, eine der schönsten Promenaden in Europa.

As a yachting mecca with its international highlight, Kiel-Week – the city promotes its image as 'sailing-city'. The naval memorial Laboe, the Olympic Centre in Schilksee, and the locks at the Kiel Canal are attractions both for visitors and the local population – as are the 'Kiellinie' and the 'Hindenburgufer', one of the most beautiful promenades in Europe.

Kieler Hauptbahnhof am Meer / Kiel, M ain Station at the sea

Landeshaus an der Förde / Parliament building at the fjord

Marine-Ehrenmal und U-Boot- Museum in Laboe / Naval memorial and Submarine Museum in Laboe

Im **Freichlichtmuseum Molfsee** vor den Toren Kiels sind in mehr als 70 Gebäuden von der Kate bis zur Mühle alle Haustypen aus der Geschichte des Bauernlandes Schleswig-Holstein aufgestellt. Sie geben einen Überblick über die ländliche Bau- und Wohnkultur in den unterschiedlichen Regionen.

Bauernhaus: Gute
Stube / farm house:
the best room

The open-air -museum Molfsee just outside Kiel displays more than 70 historical buildings. From the small cottage ('Kate') to the windmill: all the various types of houses are set up here and can be explored at leisure. Together they provide an overview of the rural style of building and living in the different regions of Schleswig-Holstein.

Bockwindmühle / Post windmill

Den idyllischen Naturraum um den **Westensee** haben einflussreiche Adlige gewählt, um dort ihre Güter zu errichten: Caspar von Saldern Schierensee, oder Fritz Reventlow Emkendorf. Um ihn und seine Frau Julia bildete sich ein Kreis von Dichtern und Gelehrten, unter ihnen Matthias Claudius, der den Salon zu einem geistigen Zentrum im 18. Jahrhundert werden ließ. Heute ist es ein beliebter Ort für Kulturveranstaltungen, wie das Schleswig-Holstein Musikfestival.

Influential noblemen chose this idyllic natural resource around the **Westensee** for their estates, like Caspar von Saldern in Schierensee, or Fritz Reventlow in Emkendorf. Together with his wife Julia, Reventlow assembled a circle of scholars and literary figures around him that made this 'salon' an intellectual centre in the 18th century. Among those taking part was Matthias Claudius. Today it is a popular place for cultural events like the Schleswig-Holstein-Music-Festival.

Eisenbahnhochbrücke und Schwebefähre
Rail bridge and hover ferry

Westensee

Emkendorf Herrenhaus / Emkendorf Manor house

Konzert im ehemaligen Kuhhaus / Concert in the former cowhouse

Die Eisenbahnbrücke über den Nord-Ostsee-Kanal mit der Schwebefähre für Personen und Autos ist das Wahrzeichen *Rendsburgs*. Über die 42 m hohe Stahlkonstruktion rollt seit 1913 der Schienenverkehr auf der Nord-Süd-Strecke. Die Altstadt war mit dem Markt, der Marienkirche und dem Schiffbrückenplatz von Ober- und Untereider umschlossen. Dänische Könige bauten die Stadt zur stärksten Festung nach Kopenhagen aus. Im Zentrum des Neuwerks liegt der große Paradeplatz, eingefasst von historischen Gebäuden. Die Christkirche bot Raum für die gesamte dänische Garnison. Das Arsenal ist heute Rendsburgs Kulturzentrum. Im Bezirk der Neustadt beherbergt die ehemalige Synagoge im Dr. Bamberger-Haus das Jüdische Museum. Die Stätte erinnert an die Juden, die sich ab 1692 in Neuwerk niederließen und vom NS-Staat vertrieben und vernichtet wurden. Ihr Friedhof in *Westerrönfeld* ist ein Kulturdenkmal. Rendsburgs wirtschaftliche Entwicklung hatte durch die Gründung der Carlshütte, den Bau des Nord-Ostsee-Kanals und die Ansiedlung der Nobiskrugwerft Impulse erfahren. Rendsburg ist mit zentralen Einrichtungen landwirtschaftlicher Mittelpunkt Schleswig-Holsteins und gehört zum Wirtschaftsraum der K.E.R.N-Region mit Kiel, Eckernförde und Neumünster.

Dr. Bamberger Haus / Dr. Bamberger House

Jüdischer Friedhof Westerrönfeld
Westerrönfeld, Jewish cemetery

Theater / Theatre

The rail bridge across the Kiel-Canal with its hover ferry for passengers and cars is the notable landmark of Rendsburg. Since 1913, the rail traffic on the north-south route has been rolling over the 42 metres high steel construction. The old part of the town with its market-place, the church of St. Mary and the 'Schiffbrückenplatz' was enclosed by the Upper and Lower Eider. Danish kings converted the town into a strong fortification second only to Copenhagen. At the centre of the 'Neuwerk', the huge 'Paradeplatz' is surrounded by historical buildings. The Church of Christ offered plenty of room for the entire Danish garrison. The 'Arsenal' is Rendsburg's cultural centre. In the region of the 'Neustadt' the former synagogue in the Dr.Bamberger House now houses the Jewish Museum. It calls to mind the situation of the Jews who from 1692 onwards settled in Neuwerk, and who were persecuted and exterminated by the Nazis. Their churchyard in Westerrönfeld bears witness to this atrocity. The opening of the 'Carlshütte', the construction of the Kiel-Canal, and the presence of the Nobiskrug shipyard in Rendsburg provided strong momentum for the economic development of the town. Due to a number of relevant institutions Rendsburg has become the agricultural centre of Schleswig-Holstein, and it also belongs to the economic merger K.E.R.N., with Kiel, Eckernförde and Neumünster as the other partners.

Marienkirche / Church of St.Mary

Altstädter Markt / Altstädter Market Place

Häuserzeile am Paradeplatz / Row of houses at the Paradeplatz

Der Missionar Vicelin gründete an der Schwale 1127 ein Stift und gab ihm den lateinischen Namen „neues Münster". Bedeutung erlangte **Neumünster** als Verkehrknotenpunkt durch den Bau der Chaussee und die Eröffnung der Bahnstrecke zwischen Kiel und Altona. Im Zuge der Industrialisierung entwickelten sich ertragreiche Tuch-, Leder-, Metall- und Papierfabriken. Ende des 2. Weltkrieges wurde der Großteil der Stadt zerstört.

In der Innenstadt sind die nach C. F. Hansen errichtete Vicelinkirche und das neugotische Rathaus auf dem zentralen Großflecken Zeugnisse aus der Vergangenheit. Die monumentale Holstenhalle ist der vielseitige Veranstaltungsort in der Messestadt Neumünster.

In 1127 the missionary Vicelin founded a religious institution close to the Schwale and gave it the Latin name for 'new minster': **Neumünster**. The town's significance lies in its function as traffic junction. The opening of the railroad track, and the construction of the carriageway from Kiel to Altona were important events for the town. In the wake of industrialization profitable cloth-, leather-, metal- and paper industries emerged. Towards the end of World War II large parts of the town were destroyed. In the inner city the church of Vicelin, built by C.F.Hansen and the neo-Gothic Town Hall in the central square (called 'Großflecken') tell of Neumünster's past. The monumental 'Holstenhalle' serves as a multi-purpose location in Neumünster with its frequent trade-fairs.

Bastion am Teich / Bastion at the pond

Reitturnier in der Holstenhalle / Horse show

Großflecken mit dem Volksfest 'Holstenköste'
Public festival

Stadthalle / City Hall

Vicelinkirche / Vicelin-Church

Jugendstilfassaden / Art Nouveau façades

Neugotisches Rathaus / Neo-Gothic Town Hall

Caspar-von-Saldern Haus / Caspar-von-Saldern House

Bad Bramstedt: Palais mit 'Roland'-Statue / Bad Bramstedt, Palace with 'Roland'statue

*Der historische Ochsenweg führte über **Bad Bramstedt**, das renommierte Rheumazentrum in der Region. Jenseits des Segeberger Forstes errichtete Kaiser Lothar 1134 die „Siegesburg", die dem Ort **Segeberg** den Namen gab. Sie diente zur Abwehr slawischer Angriffe, zur Expansion und zur Missionierung durch Vicelin. Die ehemalige Klosterkirche St. Marien ist ein Hauptwerk des mittelalterlichen Backsteinbaus im Lande.*

The historical ox-trail crossed **Bad Bramstedt**, the renowned rheumatics centre. Beyond the Segeberg-Forest Emperor Lothar built the 'Siegesburg' in 1134, which gave **Segeberg** its name. It served as a stronghold against Slavonic attacks and was also used by Vicelin during his missionary work. The former monastery church St.Mary is a major example of medieval red-brick construction in Schleswig-Holstein.

Bad Segeberg: Klosterkirche St. Marien
Bad Segeberg, Church of St. Mary

Kulisse am Fuß des Kalkbergs / Scenery at the foot of the Chalk Hill

Das Wahrzeichen von **Bad Segeberg** ist der 91 m hohe Kalkberg. Seine begehbaren Höhlen bieten Fledermäusen Quartier. Alle Informationen dazu gibt es im Zentrum „Noctalis". In das Stadion reitet Jahr für Jahr Winnetou zu den Karl-May-Spielen ein.

Bad Segeberg's best-known landmark is the 91 metres high Chalk Hill. Its caves are populated by immense numbers of bats. Information can be acquired at the 'Noctalis'- centre. Every year Winnetou comes riding into the stadium on the occasion of the Karl-May-Festival.

Bad Segeberg: Rathaus
Bad Segeberg, townhall

*Auf einem Endmoränenhügel hoch über dem Plöner See prägt das Schloss die Landschaft. In seiner Geschichte war es herzogliche Residenz, preußische Kadettenanstalt, in der auch die Söhne Kaiser Wilhelm II. erzogen wurden, Internat und im 3. Reich Nationalpolitische Erziehungsanstalt, wieder Internat und nach Verkauf und Sanierung Schulungsstätte der Fielmann-Akademie. Ein Rokoko-Juwel ist das Prinzenhaus im Schlossgarten, das für kulturelle Anlässe genutzt wird. Die mittelalterliche Stadt **Plön** ist ein touristisches Zentrum am Eingang zur holsteinischen Schweiz.*

Set high above the lake of Plön on an end-moraine-elevation, the castle clearly dominates the landscape. Historically it served as ducal residence, Prussian school for officer cadets, where also the sons of Emperor Wilhelm II were educated, then as boarding-school, during the Third Reich as Nazi educational institute, later again as boarding school, and after its sale and renovation it has now become the training centre of the Fielmann-Academy. In the garden the 'Prinzenhaus' is a veritable jewel in Rococo –style, used today for cultural events. Medieval **Plön** is a tourist attraction at the entrance to the 'Holsteinische Schweiz' (Holstein-Switzerland).

Große Plöner See Rundfahrt
Round trip Lake Plön

Schloss und Kirche / Castle and church

Selenter See: Dorf Bellin / Lake Selent: Village Bellin

In der landschaftlich reizvollen Umgebung des Selenter Sees liegen Dörfer, Herrenhäuser und Güter wie das Schloss Salzau, das als Kulturzentrum genutzt wird.

In the vicinity of Lake Selent, villages, manor houses and mansions like Castle Salzau, which today is used as a cultural centre, are typical features of the region.

Bauernhaus in der Probstei / Farm house in the Probstei

Rastorf: Herrenhaus
Rastorf, Manor house

ANNO. SOLI. DEO. GLORIA. 1723

Torhaus / Gatehouse

Am Bungsberg, mit 168 Metern die höchste Erhebung im Land, entspringt die Schwentine. Bis zur Mündung in die Kieler Förde fließt sie durch die Seenlandschaft der Holsteinischen Schweiz, durch Eutin, Bad Malente, Plön und Preetz. Am Übergang zur Probstei liegt die spätbarocke Gutsanlage Rastorf, von Dallin errichtet, mit dem Herrenhaus von C. F. Hansen.

The river Schwentine has its source at the Bungsberg, with its 168 metres the highest elevation in Schleswig-Holstein. Before it reaches its mouth in the Kiel-fjord it runs through the lake district of the 'Holsteinische Schweiz', through Eutin, Bad Malente, Plön, and Preetz. Bordering on the 'Probstei' is the late-Baroque estate Rastorf, designed by Dallin, with its manor house built by C. F. Hansen.

Gutsanlage aus dem Spätbarock / Late-Baroque estate

Herrenhaus / Manor house

*Auf der Anlage von **Gut Panker** mit dem weißen Herrenhaus, Galerien und Läden wurde 1947 ein Gestüt für die ostpreußischen Trakehner eingerichtet. Das Lieblingspferd des Fürsten von Hessenstein hat auch dem historischen Gasthof den Namen gegeben: Ole Liese.*

Panker is a typical feature of the region. On the site of Panker with its white manor house, galleries and boutiques, a stud-farm for East Prussian Trakehner-horses was founded in 1947. It was the name of the Prince of Hessenstein's favourite horse that gave its name 'Ole Liese' to the historical guesthouse on the premises.

Gasthaus „Ole Liese" / Guesthouse 'Ole Liese'

In ihrer Blütezeit galt die Stadt **Eutin** als „Weimar des Nordens". In dem Schloss mit dem englischen Landschaftsgarten residierte der Fürstbischof von Lübeck. Um seinen Hof waren Dichter wie F. L. Stolberg und der Homer-Übersetzer Voß, die Maler Tischbein und Strack versammelt. Sie hatten vielfältige Verbindungen und zogen bedeutende Zeitgenossen als Besucher an. In dieser Zeit wurde auch der Grundstein für den wertvollen Bestand der Eutiner Bibliothek gelegt. Eutin ist die Geburtsstadt Carl Maria von Webers. Bei den 1951 begründeten Festspielen auf der Naturbühne im Schlosspark steht der „Freischütz" immer wieder auf dem Spielplan. Eutin ist mit der idyllischen Landschaft um den See, der historischen Altstadt um den großen Marktplatz mit der Michaeliskirche, dem restaurierten Witwenpalais, der denkmalgeschützten Stolbergstraße ein Kleinod in der schleswig-holsteinischen Kulturlandschaft. Die Rosenstöcke vor den Häusern lassen es im Sommer erblühen.

In its time of greatest influence and prosperity towards the end of the 18th century, **Eutin** was reputed the 'Weimar of the North'. The castle with its English landscape garden was the residence of the Prince Bishop of Lübeck. In his court he gathered around him poets like F.L. Stolberg and J.H. Voß, the translator of Homer, also the painters Tischbein and Strack. They had important connexions and attracted outstanding contemporary personalities to Eutin. At that time,too, the foundation was laid for the valuable holdings of the local library. Eutin is the native town of Carl Maria von Weber, the composer of music. During the Music Festival on the open-air-stage on the castle-grounds, which was founded in 1951, von Weber's 'Freischütz' is regularly included on the programme. With its idyllic countryside around the lake, its historical town centre, the market-place, with the Church of St. Michael, the restored 'Witwenpalais' and the 'Stolbergstraße', classified as an historic site, Eutin is a veritable gem in Schleswig-Holstein's cultural scene.In summer the rose trees in front of the houses drown the town in colourful blossoms.

Stolbergstraße

Schloß: Innenhof / Castle courtyard

St. Michaelis / Church of St.Michael

Witwenpalais / Widow's Palace

Schloss / Castle

Bevor 1963 die Brücke über den Fehmarnsund eröffnet wurde, war die Insel **Fehmarn** nur über Fähren zu erreichen und entsprechend abgeschieden. Seither rollt der Transitverkehr zwischen Zentraleuropa und Skandinavien über die Vogelfluglinie. Planungen sehen statt der Fährverbindung zwischen Puttgarden und Rødby eine feste Beltquerung vor. Das Ferienzentrum Burgtiefe, vom dänischen Architekten Arne Jacobsen entworfen, ist mit seinen drei Hochhäusern ein umkämpftes Wahrzeichen auf dem Südstrand. Der Wohlstand der Bauern auf der kornreichen Insel lässt sich an der Ausstattung der Kirchen von Burg, Landkirchen und Petersdorf aus dem 13. Jahrhundert ablesen. Zwischen der Steil-, Natur- und Sandstrandküste liegen große Naturschutzgebiete. Im Wasservogelreservat Wallnau werden bis zu 250 unterschiedliche Arten von Brut- und Zugvögeln im Jahr beobachtet. Das Meereszentrum hat eines der größten Haiaquarien in Europa.

Fehmarnsundbrücke / Bridge across the Fehmarn Sound

Winterlandschaft / Winter landscape

Burgtiefe

Kirche in Petersdorf / Church in Petersdorf

Surfrevier / Surfing area

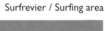

Prior to the opening of the bridge across the Fehmarn-Sound ('Fehmarnsund') in 1963, the island of **Fehmarn** could only be reached by ferry and was therefore a rather solitary place. Since then, however, transit traffic between central Europe and Scandinavia has taken its route via the 'Vogelfluglinie' (flight of birds' route). There are plans to replace the ferry service between Puttgarden and Rødby by a solid cross connection. With its three high-rise buildings, the holiday complex 'Burgtiefe', planned by the Danish architect Arne Jacobsen, is a controversial landmark on the southern beach. The interiors of the churches in Burg, the country-churches and 'Petersdorf' dating back to the 13th century bear witness to the prosperity of the corn-farmers on the island. Between steep cliff banks and the natural sandy coast extensive areas of land have been declared protected areas. Up to 250 different species of hatching birds and birds of passage can be watched in the water-bird-reserve Wallnau. The marine-centre holds one of the biggest shark–aquariums in Europe.

Neustadt: Pagodenspeicher / Neustadt, Pagoda storehouse

Neustadt ist von Adolf IV. auf dem gleichen Grundriss angelegt worden wie Kiel. Die Hafenstadt war der zentrale Handelsort für die ländliche Umgebung. Direkt an den Hafen grenzt der Marktplatz mit der Stadtkirche aus dem Gründungsjahr 1244. Hier wird das europäische Folklorefestival veranstaltet. Vor Neustadt wurde am 3.Mai 1945 im Luftangriff die „Cap Arcona" mit 7000 Häftlingen aus dem KZ Neuengamme versenkt. An das Unglück erinnert ein Denkmal auf dem Ehrenfriedhof.

Neustadt was laid out by Adolf IV along the same ground-plan as Kiel. The sea-port was the principal trading post for the rural neighbourhood. Directly adjacent to the harbour is the market-place with the City Church, dating from the year of its foundation 1244. Here the European Festival of Folklore is held. Just outside Neustadt the Cap Arcona with 7000 prisoners from the Neuengamme concentration camp was sunk during an air attack on March 3, 1945. A memorial in the cemetery is reminiscent of this catastrophe.

Hafen und Kirche / Harbour and church

Hasselburg: Gutsanlage / Hasselburg, Estate

Der Kreis Ostholstein ist reich an Bodendenkmalen aus der Zeit der slawischen Besiedlung: der Burgwall des Hauptortes Oldenburg mit dem Museum ist dafür ein Zeugnis. Die Region ist aber auch historische Gutslandschaft. Die spätbarocke Anlage **Hasselburg** in Altenkrempe mit der repräsentativen Festhalle gehört zu den eindrucksvollsten Beispielen. Sie wird zu festlichen kulturellen Anlässen genutzt.

The district Ostholstein is rich with archaeological finds from the time of the Slavonic settlement. The castle mound of the main town Oldenburg with its museum bears witness here. However, the region is also the historical setting for manor houses. **Hasselburg** in Altenkrempe with its prestigious Festival Hall is among the most impressive examples. It is used for festive cultural events.

Hasselburg: Großscheune / Hasselburg, Big barn

Hasselburg: Torhaus / Hasselburg, Gatehouse

Hasselburg: Herrenhaus / Hasselburg, Manor house

Neben den nordfriesischen Inseln und der holsteinischen Schweiz ist die Lübecker Bucht die gefragteste Ferienregion des Landes.
An dem Küstenstreifen mit feinen Sandstränden liegen beliebte Bäder wie Haffkrug/Scharbeutz, Dahme, Grömitz und **Timmendorfer Strand**. Der Badeort hat sich als Kongress- und Tagungszentrum etabliert. Seit der Öffnung der deutsch-deutschen Grenze steht das Gebiet in Konkurrenz zu den Ferienorten an der mecklenburgischen und pommerschen Küste.

Next to the North Frisian islands and the 'Holsteinische Schweiz' the bay of Lübeck is the most important holiday region in Schleswig-Holstein. Along the coast-line with its attractive sandy beaches, such widely favoured resorts as Dahme, Grömitz, Haffkrug, Scharbeutz, and **Timmendorfer Strand** have increasingly become popular among holidaymakers. Timmendorf has managed to develop into a well-established congress- and conference-centre. Since the opening of the border between the two German states the region has entered into strong competition with the coastal area of Mecklenburg and Pomerania.

Brodtner Steilufer / Brodtner steep coast

Timmendorfer Strand / Timmendorf-Beach

Travemünde hat als erstes Ostseebad eine über 200 Jahre alte Tradition. Mit seinen eleganten Villen, Kurhaus und Casino wurde es zur Sommerfrische der europäischen Gesellschaft. Dostojewski, Gogol, Turgenjew, Kafka, Edvard Munch, Richard Wagner und natürlich Thomas Mann promenierten hier, der Kaiser eröffnete die 1. Travemünder Woche. Sie ist bis heute eine segelsportliche Attraktion. Der Fährschiffhafen ist einer der größten in Europa.

Badekarre / Changing cubicle

Travemünde: Kurhaus / Travemünde, Spa house

As the first seaside resort on the Baltic, **Travemünde** has a 200-year-old tradition. With its elegant mansions, spa rooms, and casino it has become the summer resort of European society. Dostoevski, Gogol, Turgenev, Kafka, E.Munch, Richard Wagner and – of course - Thomas Mann leisurely walked the streets here.
The Emperor himself opened the first Travemünde Week. Since then this week has been a maritime attraction and sailing event. The ferry terminal ist one of the biggest in Europe.

Casino

Hotel-Hochhaus und Leuchtturm
Multi-storey hotel building and lighthouse

Museumsschiff „Passat"
Museum ship 'Passat'

Die sieben Kirchtürme, die weithin die Stadtsilhouette bestimmen, und das Holstentor sind die Wahrzeichen von **Lübeck**. *Über die Puppenbrücke führt der Weg in die Altstadt, an der sich die Geschichte ablesen lässt: von den Anfängen und der 2. Gründung durch Heinrich den Löwen, über die Blüte an der Spitze der Hanse bis zur Zerstörung im 2. Weltkrieg, bei der in der Nacht zum Palmsonntag 1942 ein Fünftel der Altstadt den Bomben zum Opfer fiel, und dem Wiederaufbau bis in die Gegenwart.*

Puppenbrücke: Figur
des Merkur

Dolls' Bridge, figure
of Mercury

The seven church spires which dominate the city's silhouette and the 'Holstentor' (Holsten-Gate) are well-known **Lübeck** landmarks. Across the 'Puppenbrücke' (Doll's Bridge) the road leads directly to the old centre of the town, where Lübeck's history can be traced back from its beginnings and the second foundation by Henry the Lion, via its top position at the head of the Hanseatic League – right through to the destruction in World War II. In 1942, during the night preceding Palm Sunday, one fifth of the old part of the town fell victim to the bombs.

Das historische Lübeck / the historical side of Lübeck

Salzspeicher / Salt storehouse

Das historische Lübeck zwischen Trave und Wakenitz ist seit 1987 Teil des Weltkulturerbes der UNESCO. Es umfasst das gesamte Stadtbild mit seinen Straßenzügen, den Fassaden von der Romanik bis zum Jugendstil; die repräsentativen Giebelhäuser; die Stiftungshöfe-restaurierte Wohnoasen wie die Anlagen im typischen Gängeviertel. Hier liegen Museen, das Stadttheater und traditionelle Kunsthandwerkerbetriebe. Die Lübecker Musikhochschule hat ein ganzes Quartier an der Untertrave bezogen.

Siebente Querstraße / Seventh Side Road

Reconstruction followed, and since 1987 historic Lübeck between the rivers Trave and Wakenitz has been part of UNESCO's world cultural heritage. It includes the entire municipal district with its old streets, façades that date from the times of Romanticism and Art Nouveau – 'Jugendstil' – the imposing gabled houses, the 'Stiftungshöfe' and restored peaceful residential housing areas like the typical 'Gängeviertel'. Here is the centre of museums, the municipal theatre, of cozy pubs and arts and crafts galleries. Lübeck's Music School has taken up quarters along the 'Untertrave'.

Schiffergesellschaft / Skippers' Company

Buddenbrook-Haus / Buddenbrook-House

Rathaus / Town Hall

Musikhochschule / Academy of Music

Die Altstadt hat viele Prunkstücke: das mittelalterliche Heilig-Geist-Hospital, das Burgkloster und die Kirchen. Die gewichtigste ist der Dom, für den Heinrich der Löwe den Grundstein gesetzt hat. Der gotische Backsteinbau mit dem wertvollen Inventar, wie dem Triumphkreuz von Bernd Notke, wurde nach der Zerstörung aufwendig restauriert. Das Rathaus und die Marienkirche sind Zeugnisse des Selbstbewusstseins von Rat und Bürgerschaft, das auf wirtschaftlichem Erfolg, politischer Macht und weltweitem Ansehen beruhte.

'Schöne Madonna' von 1509
Beautiful Madonna

Dom: Triumphkreuz / Cathedral: Cross of Triumph

The old part of the town prides itself with a number of attractions such as the medieval Heilig-Geist-Hospital, the monastery ('Burgkloster'), and its churches. The most impressive one is the Cathedral, which was initiated by Henry the Lion. This Gothic red-brick edifice with its precious interior design – like Bernd Notke's 'Cross of Triumph' – has been elaborately restored after its destruction in the war. Both the Town Hall and the Church of St. Mary are still bearing witness to the self-assurance of the town-council and the citizens, which was based on economic prosperity, political power, and world-wide esteem.

Dom zu Lübeck / Cathedral

Marienkirche: Kapelle mit herabgestürzten Glocken
Church of St.Mary: Chapel with bells that fell down during an air-raid

Blick auf die Kirchtürme / View of the church towers

Lübeck ist die Kulturhauptstadt des Landes. Sie ist die Literaturstadt, die mit Thomas Mann und Günter Grass gleich zwei Nobelpreisträger beheimatet; Musikstadt, in der Buxtehude wirkte, und auch Standort bedeutender Museen, die die Kunst des Mittelalters bis zur Gegenwart präsentieren.

Lübeck is the cultural centre of Schleswig-Holstein. In the field of literature it is the home of two Nobel-Prize winners, Thomas Mann and Günter Grass. Buxtehude composed music here.

Marienkirche / Church of St.Mary

Heilig-Geist-Hospital / Holy Ghost-Hospital

Kirchenhalle / Church hall

Niederegger-Stammhaus
Niederegger parent company

Lübeck ist in der Mischung von Tradition und Moderne ein Gesamtkunstwerk. Rotspon und Marzipan sind in der Welt bekannte Botschafter.

Lübeck is the site of influential museums which dedicate themselves to medieval as well as modern art.

Rathausmarkt / Town Hall market place

Musik- und Kongresshalle / Music and Congress Hall

Turm der Petrikirche
Tower of St.Petri

Der alte Handelsweg Lübeck-Hamburg quert die Trave bei der früheren Salzstadt Bad Oldesloe im Kreis Storman. Zu den Sehenswürdigkeiten der Region gehört das **Schloss Ahrensburg**, das als Museum mit wertvollem Interieur die Adelskultur des Landes präsentiert. Zur gleichen Zeit entstand **Reinbek.** Wie Kiel, Husum und Tönning war es ein landesherrliches Schloss, von Herzog Adolf gebaut. Es wurde restauriert und als Kulturzentrum eingerichtet.

Das Kloster Reinbek war in der Geschichte der südlichste Grenzpunkt des Dänischen Königreichs. Der anschließende Sachsenwald ist das größte zusammenhängende Forstgebiet des waldarmen Landes Schleswig-Holstein. Der Reichskanzler Otto von Bismarck hatte ihn nach dem Sieg über Frankreich und der Reichsgründung zum Geschenk erhalten. Er ist in **Friedrichsruh** begraben.

In dem Museum ist u.a. sein Arbeitszimmer eingerichtet, im historischen Bahnhofsgebäude wird Bismarcks Nachlass verwaltet. Eine touristische Attraktion ist der **Schmetterlingsgarten**.

Schloss Ahrensburg / Ahrensburg Castle

Schloss Reinbek / Reinbek Castle

The old transit route Lübeck – Hamburg crosses the river Trave near the former salt-mining town Bad Oldesloe in the district of Stormarn. Castle Ahrensburg, a museum that exhibits valuable interior designs, is just one of the attractions in this region. Reinbek was built roughly at the same time. Like Kiel, Husum, and Tönning it was a sovereign prince's castle, initiated by Duke Adolf. It has been restored and turned into a cultural centre.

Friedrichsruh: Bismarck-Museum

In the past Monastery Reinbek was the southernmost point of the Danish kingdom. Adjacent to it the Sachsenwald is the largest coherent forest area in this region that otherwise is only scarcely endowed with woodland. It was donated to Chancellor of the Reich Otto von Bismarck on the occasion of his victory over France and the foundation of the German Reich. Von Bismarck lies buried in Friedrichsruh. Among various exhibits in the local museum his study-room can be seen there. In the historic rail-station building his estate is today being administered. The butterfly garden is another tourist attraction of the area.

Schmetterlingsgarten / Butterfly garden

Wichtig für die Hansestädte Hamburg und Lübeck war die Transitstrecke durch das Herzogtum Lauenburg, über die der Salzhandel von Lüneburg an die Ostsee abgewickelt wurde. Der Bau des **Stecknitz-Kanals** zwischen Elbe und Trave, später als Elbe-Lübeck-Kanal ausgebaut, förderte die Region. An der Trasse Lübeck- Ratzeburg verlief die innerdeutsche **Grenze**, die das mecklenburgische Hinterland abgetrennt hatte.

For the Hanseatic cities of Hamburg and Lübeck the transit route across the Duchy of Lauenburg used to be of vital importance, as along it happened the salt trade from Lüneburg to the Baltic. The construction of the Stecknitz-Canal between the rivers Elbe and Trave, later extended and re-named Elbe-Lübeck-Canal came as a welcome boost for the region. Along the route from Lübeck to Ratzeburg the border between the two German states separated the Mecklenburg hinterland from Schleswig-Holstein.

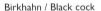
Birkhahn / Black cock

Naturlandschaft im ehemaligen Grenzstreifen
Unspoilt nature at the former border-line

Alter DDR-Grenzpfahl / Old boundary post

*Der Dom, der in **Ratzeburg** die Insel mit der Altstadt überragt, ist die erste monumentale Backsteinkirche Norddeutschlands. Heinrich der Löwe hat das Bistum gegründet. Das slawische Gebiet war lange umkämpft. Bei einem der Überfalle wurde der Abt Ansverus vom Kloster St. Georg gesteinigt. An ihn erinnert das Ansverus-Kreuz in Einhaus. Der idyllische Domhof mit dem Kreuzgang und Friedhof, dem spätbarocken Herrenhaus und dem A. Paul Weber-Museum bildet ein historisches Ensemble, das in dem Marktplatz mit der klassizistischen St.Petri-Kirche und dem Barlach-Museum eine Entsprechung findet. Der Ratzeburger See ist international als Ruderstrecke berühmt. Freizeitsportler und Ausflügler haben im Naturpark Lauenburgische Seen ein abwechslungsreiches Revier.*

The Cathedral that in **Ratzeburg** towers above the island with the old part of the town is the oldest red-brick monumental edifice in the north of Germany. It was Henry the Lion who founded the diocese. For a long time the Slavonic region used to be disputed territory. In the course of one of the raids, Abbot Ansverus of the Monastery St. George was stoned to death. The Ansverus-Cross in Einhaus stands in commemoration of this sad event. The idyllic cathedral court with its cross vault and graveyard, with its late-Baroque mansion and the A. Paul Weber-Museum –

all these together form an historic ensemble that finds its equivalent in the market-place with its classical Church of St. Petri and the Barlach museum. Ratzeburg's lake has won world-wide renown as a rowing centre .Fans of recreational sport and day-trippers can find a variety of interesting opportunities in the Nature Park 'Lauenburgische Seen'.

Backsteingotik
Red-brick Gothic style

Denkmal Heinrichs des Löwen / Memorial of Henry the Lion

Ratzeburger See und Dom / Lake Ratzeburg and Cathedral

*Zwischen Seen und Wäldern ist die Stadt **Mölln** eingebettet. Sie war als Opfer der Machtkämpfe im Herzogtum Lauenburg von 1359 an über mehr als 300 Jahre an Lübeck verpfändet. Die malerische Altstadt des Luftkurorts wird vom gotischen Backsteinbau des Rathauses und der Nikolaikirche bestimmt. An ihrem Westportal ist der Gedenkstein an Till Eulenspiegel eingemauert. Der Possenreißer ist seit dem 16.Jahrhundert eine über Europa verbreitete literarische Figur. Das Buch von seinen Streichen ist in über 280 Sprachen übersetzt. Der Überlieferung nach soll er in Mölln begraben sein.*

Mölln: Nikolaikirche / Mölln, Church of St.Nikolai

Eulenspiegel / Jester Eulenspiegel

For more than 300 years, beginning in 1359, **Mölln** was pledged to Lübeck, due to the struggles for power in the Duchy of Lauenburg. Nestling among lovely woods and lakes the picturesque old part of this health resort today displays its Gothic brick Town Hall and the Church of St. Nikolai. At its western entrance the statue of Till Eulenspiegel can be seen. Since the 16th century this jester has been a literary figure throughout Europe. The book, relating his merry pranks, has been translated into more than 280 languages. Legend has it that he lies buried in Mölln.

Zunftschild / Guild-plaque

Palmschleuse / Kettle lock

Raddampfer 'Kaiser Wilhelm / Paddle-steamer

*Mölln liegt am Stecknitz-Kanal, der ältesten künstlichen Wasserstraße Deutschlands. Über 500 Jahre transportierten flache Kähne das kostbare Handelsgut Salz aus Lüneburg in die Lübecker Speicher; dann wurde die Verbindung durch den Elbe-Lübeck-Kanal abgelöst. Ausgangspunkt ist die Stadt **Lauenburg**. Die Palmschleuse ist die älteste Kesselschleuse Europas und ein technisches Denkmal. Die Schiffersiedlung wurde zur Residenz der Herzöge Sachsen-Lauenburg, die in der Maria-Magdalenen-Kirche bestattet sind. Am Steilufer der Elbe teilt sich der Ort in Ober- und Unterstadt. Sie ist mit ihren reizvollen Fachwerkhäusern vom Hochwasser bedroht. Lauenburg war Verkehrsknotenpunkt an einer der wichtigsten Handelsstraßen des Nordens. Heute ist es ein zentraler Ort an den Ländergrenzen von Schleswig-Holstein, Mecklenburg-Vorpommern, Niedersachsen und Hamburg.*

Mölln is situated on the Stecknitz-Canal, Germany's oldest man-made waterway. For more than 500 years flat-bottomed barges transported salt, a precious and expensive merchandise, from Lübeck to the silos in Lübeck. Later this link was replaced by the Elbe-Lübeck-Canal. Starting point is **Lauenburg**. The 'Palmschleuse' is the oldest kettle lock in Europe and as such also a technical relic and monument. The 'Schiffersiedlung' (Skippers' Area) was later turned into the residence of the Dukes of Saxe-Lauenburg, who lie buried in the Church of Maria-Magdalena. The steep banks of the Elbe mark the dividing line between Upper- and Lower Town.. The latter with its attractive half-timbered houses is in danger of being flooded. Lauenburg was a central traffic junction on one of the busiest trade routes in the north. Today it is an important site on the borderline of Schleswig-Holstein, Mecklenburg - Western Pomerania, Lower Saxony and Hamburg.

Lauenburg: Blick vom niedersächsischen Ufer / Lauenburg, View from the Lower-Saxon bank

Register

zu den Autoren / about the authors

Brigitte Schubert-Riese, Dr. phil.
Studium Germanistik/Geschichte an der CAU Kiel.
Journalistin, Redakteurin des Norddeutschen Rundfunks.
(1967-1989 Landesfunkhaus Kiel, 1989-2002 NDR 3 Hamburg).
Veröffentlichungen zu Themen der Kulturgeschichte.

Studies in German and History at Kiel-University.
Journalist, editor with Radio NDR: 1967-1989 Studio Kiel;
1989 – 2002 NDR 3 Studio Hamburg.
Publications in the field of cultural history.

Peter Schuster
geboren 1940 in Kiel, Bundesmarine, Verlagskaufmann
Autor und Co-Autor mehrerer Bücher, Bildbände und Zooführer.
Fotografiert als Autodidakt, arbeitet für den Wachholtz-Verlag seit 1981,
freier Bildautor seit seiner Pensionierung

Born 1940 in Kiel, Federal Navy, publishing specialist.
Author and co-author of various books, volumes of photography and guides to zoological gardens.
Self-taught photographer, since 1981 work for Wachholtz publishing house.
Today, after retirement, freelance photographer.

Günter Schubert
Anglist. Lehrtätigkeit am Gymnasium.
Von 1977 bis 2001 Studienleiter am Institut für Praxis und Theorie der Schule (IPTS) in Kiel,
Fachberater für das Fach Englisch an Gymnasien und beruflichen Schulen.
Veröffentlichungen von Unterrichtsmaterialien, Mitarbeit an Lehrbüchern.

After graduation from Kiel University English teacher at a grammar school.
Teacher trainer at the IPTS (teacher training and in-service institute) in Kiel from 1977-2001.
Adviser for English at secondary- and vocational schools.
Publications of teaching materials and co-author of text-books.